HISTORY,

HILARITY AND

HEARTBREAK

Sedona stories...and more

By Loretta Benore

Published by Sedona Heritage Publishing, held by the Sedona Historical Society, Inc.

Visit Our Website

  www.sedonamuseum.org

Like us on Facebook

Facebook.com/sedonamuseum

View Our Calendar of Events

  Sedonamuseum.org/calendar

Printed in the United States of America

Cover Photo by William Levengood

ISBN: 978-1542565943

ACKNOWLEDGEMENTS

I would like to thank Beth Lanzoni for convincing me to put this book together and coming up with the title. My husband David for the many modern photos he took and for all the computer work. It goes without saying that without the archives of the Sedona Historical Society this book would not have been possible. Finally, I would like to thank Bill Levengood for putting this book together and ready for publication.

Table of Contents

UNIQUE ARIZONA

The folks in Arizona have always marched to their own drummer. For instance, in 1861 the citizens got tired of being ignored by the Feds in D.C. and passed an "Ordinance of Secession" to secede from the Union. In February, 1862, Jefferson Davis, president of the Confederacy, recognized Arizona as an official Territory of the Confederate States of America. The Feds in D.C. had a hissy fit, woke up to realize that the Johnny Rebs would have a direct route through the South to the gold fields of California, and in February, 1863, made Arizona an official Territory of the United States.

Arizona supposedly was the location of the Seven Cities of Gold whose streets were paved with gold-plate and whose hammers and hoes were made of precious metals. The king of Spain sent Francisco Coronado off to the New World to find these fabled cities and to bring back the gold. The raping of the American West for its precious metals had begun.

Every state has its state trees, flowers, mottos, etc. But Arizona was the first state to have an Official State Neck Tie. The bolo tie, one of the most original American fashion styles, is not a creation of the Old West. Its invention (and exploitation) goes back only to the mid-twentieth century. The story goes...In the 1940s, Victor Cedarstaff went riding in the Bradshaw Mountains when a strong wind blew his hat off. He grabbed the hat and removed the hatband — which had a silver buckle — putting it around his neck. His friends who were with him complimented him on his new necktie (tongue in cheek?) An idea was born! At home he wove a leather string, added silver balls to the ends, and ran it through a turquoise buckle. At last! A necktie that did not choke the wearer. Cedarstaff named it a bolo tie after the boleadora — lariat — that Argentine gauchos used to catch cattle and game. He patented it, and a new fashion fad exploded.

Early in the twentieth century, after much politicking, the Federal government agreed to consider Arizona for statehood. Arizona's constitutional convention in 1910-11 included such novel reforms as referendum, recall, initiative, women's suffrage, and the direct election of senators. President Taft, whose dream it was to become a Supreme Court Judge (his wife wanted him to be president), objected to the recall clause...it would allow the recall of judges. The offending clauses were removed. On February 14, 1912, Arizona was officially granted statehood. At the next state convention, each one of the offending clauses was put back into the state constitution!

Of necessity, Arizona and its citizens were (and still are) unique in their ability to think outside the box. The settlers in and around Red Rock Country bear that out. They came out to this spot of nowhere (admittedly beautiful), settled, and prospered. There really must be something magical about it since we're all here, and the name Sedona and Red Rock Country is recognized in much of the world.

I hope you will enjoy these stories about Sedona and the 48th state...and maybe learn a little something you did not know about this magical, mystical area we call home.

BEFORE THE RED ROCKS

Do you ever ponder what it was like here in the days of *really, really* yore, before golf courses and housing developments. . .before dusty trails and ranches. . .before the red rocks? Until recently there has been very little archeological and not much more geological information specific to the Red Rock Country in print. Certainly, there have been papers and journal articles presented by learned earth scientists, but there hasn't been much that an ordinary individual could read and understand about the birth of Red Rock Country.

Recently I stumbled across a fascinating little book, geared to the average reader, that brings to life the unique beginning of these awesome red rocks. Wayne Ranney, in his book *Sedona Through Time*, answers many of these questions.

What is unique about the setting? Sedona (and Big Park) not only straddles two county lines—Yavapai and Coconino, it also straddles two geological provinces—the Colorado Plateau and the Transition Zone (transitioning from the high plateau country in the north to Basin and Range country in the south). Its red rocks are related to the rocks of the Mogollon Rim.

Why are the rocks red? There is a thin coating of iron oxide (rust) on the outside of each individual grain of sand that makes up the rocks.

Was the Sedona area always this dramatic with towering rocks, mesas and escarpments? No, not at all. At one time the area was a broad river floodplain, later it was a huge Sahara-like desert, then it was at the bottom of an ancient sea. Over millions of years, mountains thrust up and eroded away; seas formed and disappeared, while the continents and collided and broke apart. The geological history of Red Rock Country is traced from 350 million years ago to one million years ago.

What about volcanoes? Were there any here? Most people would be amazed to learn that we here in the Village are living on the slope of a volcano. It isn't a dramatically erupting mountain like Mt. Fuji, but House Mountain (immediately southwest of the Village) is a shield volcano. Shield volcanoes ooze very fluid lava for many miles in all directions when they erupt. Intensive study of this mountain began only in the 1980s. At first, it was believed to be about 5.5 million years old. But the mountain held a little mystery that belied this. More investigation revealed that House Mountain volcano lay beneath the ancestral Mogollon Rim. Lava flowed only to the east, south, and west. The Rim blocked any lava flow to the north. As the Rim receded to its present location (it's still receding at the rate of one foot every 625 years) Big Park was formed. Based on this information, it is estimated that House Mountain is about 14.5 million years old and is resting quietly.

ARIZONA – THE TERRITORY

In February 2012 Arizona celebrated its 100th anniversary as a state. But when one takes a look at its territorial history, it is amazing that it ever made it to statehood.

As a result of the Gadsden Purchase in 1853/1854, what is now southern Arizona became one with New Mexico. Although the size of this combined territory spoke to a need to separate the territory of Arizona from the territory of New Mexico, Congress was loathe to create this separation along an east-west border. The Civil War was looming. Legislators believed that folks in the western part of the New Mexico Territory were southern sympathizers (they were right), but could be kept at bay if Arizona was not a separate territory. In 1861, the Confederate Army successfully took possession of this territory, running east-west with its northern border along the 34th parallel [about the northern border of present day Maricopa County], in the name of the Confederacy. Arizona Territory then seceded from the Union. In 1862, the southern sympathizing population of the territory officially declared that it was part of the Confederacy. And on February 14, 1862, the Confederate Territory of Arizona was officially created by President Jefferson Davis.

Congress realized this was a big "OOPS." The Confederacy now had a direct route through friendly territory to California and its gold. A big rush was made to remedy this situation, and in 1863, the bill establishing the Arizona Territory with an eastern border along the 107th meridian was passed by the House, the Senate, and signed by President Lincoln. This Act was the Organic Act of Arizona Territory.

Then came the effort to create a territorial government. Ohioan John Gurley was appointed governor, but died before he could actually take office. John Goodwin of Maine was named governor in his place. Now all these easterners just needed to get to this territory they were overseeing. Easier said than done.

In September of 1863 the Territorial party headed out to Arizona. They separated into two groups, one coming through Yuma under military escort, and one through Kansas roughly along the Santa Fe Trail. The first group headed to Tucson, mistakenly thinking that was to be the capital. The second group took the wrong road and got lost less than 10 miles from their starting point. Finally, by December 29, they all found their way inside the territory and officially organized the government of Arizona.

Arizona has had "interesting" governors. John Gurley died before getting here. John Goodwin got lost getting here; Richard McCormick was a newspaperman who brought his wife here. Anson Safford actually granted himself a divorce. John Charles Fremont had been an explorer, a governor of California, a senator from California, a general in the Union Army. He legalized gambling in the Territory, and started a lottery to pay for public buildings and schools. Conrad Zulick was held in a Mexican jail at the time of his appointment, but would later sign the order moving the capital from Prescott to Phoenix. Lewis Wolfley established what would become the "Arizona Republic" to further his political ends. Arizona was finally on its long road to statehood.

THE BIRTH OF A TERRITORY

Arizona's birth as a territory did not come easy. The labor pains were long and fitful. They began in 1853 when the Gadsden Purchase expanded the New Mexico Territory by 45,500 square miles. This land encompassed what is now southern New Mexico and southern Arizona. Because of the size of the New Mexico Territory and the problem with effective territorial government, attempts to create a separate territory began as early as 1856. These early attempts failed. For good reason, the U. S. Congress was loathe to separate Arizona from the territory of New Mexico along an east-west border. Speculation was that since the country was almost in the throes of Civil War, some federal legislators were of the opinion that folks in the western part of the New Mexico Territory were southern sympathizers (they were right), but could be kept impotent if Arizona was not organized as a separate territory. In 1861, Lt. Col. John Baylor of the Confederate Army successfully assaulted Ft. Fillmore in Mesilla and took possession of this territory, running east-west with its northern border along the 34th parallel [about the northern border of present day Maricopa County], in the name of the Confederacy. At this time, the Arizona territory seceded from the Union. In 1862, the southern sympathizing population of the territory officially declared that it was part of the Confederacy. And on February 14, 1862, the Confederate Territory of Arizona was officially created by President Jefferson Davis.

Meanwhile, in Washington, D.C., the U. S. Congress is saying "OOPS." The Confederacy now had a direct route through friendly territory to California and its gold as well as the newly discovered gold in Prescott. It was through the unwavering efforts of Charles Poston, known as the "Father of Arizona," that the bill establishing the Arizona Territory with a north-south border along the 107th meridian was passed by the House, then finally passed by the Senate in February of 1863. President Lincoln signed the bill four days later. This Act, jointly sponsored by Watts of New Mexico and Ashley of Ohio, would become the Organic Act of Arizona Territory. The measure was strongly pushed by mining interests in the Midwest, especially Ohio. Lobbying by special corporate interests – golly gee!

Poor Charles Poston. In some ways, he was a 19th century version of Rodney Dangerfield – he just didn't get any respect. After all his work lobbying Congressional members, when the territorial officers were appointed, through an oversight, he was omitted from the list. Only after it was brought to the attention of the newly named governor of the territory, Ohioan John Gurley, was Poston given a position in the territorial government. He was named Indian Agent. Still, he came out better than Governor Gurley, who died shortly after being appointed, but before he could actually take office. John Goodwin of Maine was named governor in his place. Now all these easterners just needed to get to this territory they were overseeing. Easier said than done.

In September of 1863 the territorial party finally began its westward trek to Arizona. (By the way, there is still disagreement among historians about the origin of the name Arizona. The most popular definitions are: (1) a Tohono O'odham word "arizonac" meaning place of little springs; (2) a Spanish phrase "arida zona" meaning arid zone; (3) an Aztec word "arizuma" meaning silver bearing. Take your choice.) The group did not travel as a single party. Charles Poston was one member of the segment that entered the territory through Yuma under a military escort. They headed on to Tucson, not realizing that a change had been made in the location of the Territorial Capital and they should have headed on to Fort Whipple, near present Prescott. (The federal government did not name the territorial capital, but allowed the governor and legislature to locate the seat of government. General James Carleton then convinced the powers that be that Tucson was full of secessionists and did not deserve to be the Territorial Capital.)

The other segment, which included the newly appointed Governor John Goodwin, the Secretary of State, the Chief Justice, the District Attorney, Surveyor General and the newly appointed Postmaster of the Arizona Territory left Leavenworth, Kansas, and was to travel by military roads and forts to Pawnee Rock on the Santa Fe Trail. The wagon train was accompanied by Companies of the Missouri Cavalry and the Missouri Militia. Documents from the Kansas State Historical Society noted them to be incompetent and compared them unfavorably to Quantrill's Raiders. The Cavalry led the train which stretched out for over a mile. There was no guide because, supposedly, it was impossible to get off the trail. The impossible became very possible. As the wagon train moved on without a real guide, the trail somehow dwindled and disappeared. Wagons overturned and were damaged. They found only isolated farmhouses. There was no going forward. The Company had to partly retrace its way in an attempt to find the main road. Since it would have been a terrific loss of face to show up back in Leavenworth two days after they set out, the men chose to take down fences and scramble to get back to the road without actually returning to Leavenworth. They had gotten lost less than 10 miles from their starting point. That did not bode well for their journey to the unknown southwest and that desert frontier known as Arizona.

Fortunately, the next several months of their journey through Kansas, Colorado, and New Mexico were more successful. Finally, near the end of December, the party moved on to Zuni Pueblo through a blinding snowstorm. They thought they had crossed the Arizona line, but were not sure. So they went on for another 40 miles in another snowstorm to Navajo Springs (about 20 miles northeast of the Petrified Forest) to be absolutely sure that they were really in the new territory before officially establishing its government. It was critical that they be in the legal boundaries of the territory as soon as possible, as Congress had stipulated that none of them would be paid until they were working on Arizona soil. It was here on December 29, they began the ceremony of organization for the government of Arizona. The oath of office was administered to the officials, the governor's proclamation was read, the flag was raised. On the pre-written proclamation, the name Navajo Springs and the date December 29, 1863 had to be inserted. However, they also wrote in the proclamation that the seat of government for the present would be at or near Fort Whipple. Arizona was now, finally, an official territory of the United States of America.

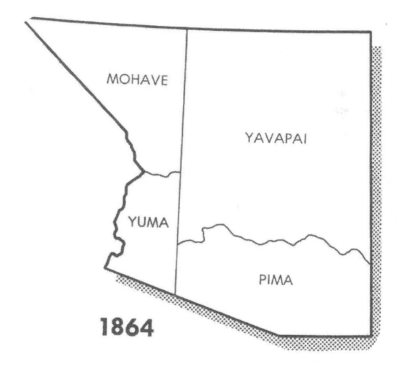

YAVAPAI – THE INCREDIBLE SHRINKING COUNTY

With the Arizona Territory a reality, the business of government could actually get under way. Governor John Goodwin called an election for July 18, 1864 to select members for the First Territorial Legislature, for a delegate to Congress, and for local officers. Three Judicial Districts had been established for the new Territory, and these Districts were named as voting districts with voting precincts. The First Judicial District comprised everything south of the Gila and east of present Yuma County. The Second Judicial District included what later became Mohave and Yuma Counties. The Third Judicial District comprised all the rest of the Territory.

Following the election—in which Indian Agent Charles Debrille Poston finally got some respect and was elected as the Territory's first delegate to the U.S. Congress—the First Territorial Legislature met in Prescott in September to create the original four counties of Arizona. Pima County coincided with the First Judicial District; Mohave and Yuma Counties were created from the Second Judicial District; and Yavapai County coincided with the Third Judicial District. Yavapai was named after the Yavapai Indians, which means "hill people" or "people of the sun," depending on which source you use. Another questionable source suggests Yavapai means "all mouth" or "talking people." The Yavapai people, who certainly should know, refer to themselves as "People of the Sun."

Poor Charlie Poston's ill luck continued. His leisurely trip to take his seat in Congress, going from Arizona to Washington, D.C. via Panama, has been cited as the first questionable and unnecessary Congressional junket, $7000 in 1864 dollars. He served from December,

1864 to March, 1865, when he was removed from office by the electorate!

When Yavapai County was created, it comprised more than 65,000 square miles. It constituted an area more than one-half the entire Arizona territory, and it was practically equal in size to all of New England. In fact, the majority of Arizona's present fourteen counties were taken fully or partly from the original Yavapai County. For a very good reason, Yavapai is known as "The Mother of Counties."

Yavapai's progeny were born in the following order: Maricopa County, in its original form, was spawned from Yavapai County in 1871; however, Maricopa later bit off the Gila Bend area from Pima County. Thus, present-day Maricopa was taken mainly from Yavapai and partly from Pima Counties. Apache County was taken from Yavapai in 1879, from which Navajo County was later formed. Gila County was spun off from Yavapai in 1881. Coconino County took a huge chunk from Yavapai County in 1891. The step-children of Yavapai County (partially created from Old Yavapai or from counties originally taken from her) include Pinal, Graham, and Greenlee. Actually, three of Yavapai's children have outgrown their mother in size. Coconino County is more than twice the size of her mother at 18,573 square miles. (Only San Bernadino County in California is larger, with 20,130 square miles.) Apache County is at 11,174 square miles, and Navajo County is at 9,991 square miles.

However, Yavapai County, at 8,125 square miles (only 12.5 percent of its original size) still holds up pretty well. It is larger than either Massachusetts or New Jersey. And it is larger than the combined areas of Rhode Island, Connecticut and Delaware.

The U. S. Forest Service owns 38 percent of the land in Yavapai County, including parts of Tonto, Coconino, and Prescott national forests. The State of Arizona owns another 25 percent. About eleven percent is BLM land, and 25 percent is individually or corporately owned. The Yavapai Indian Reservation and public lands occupy only about one percent of the county.

Remember the hapless Charlie Poston—sometimes known (questionably) as the "Father of Arizona"? His bad luck continued. Although he received a commission to study irrigation practices in Asia and Europe, passed the bar and practiced law, was a land office registrar in Florence, a consular agent in El Paso, he still died penniless in Phoenix in 1902.

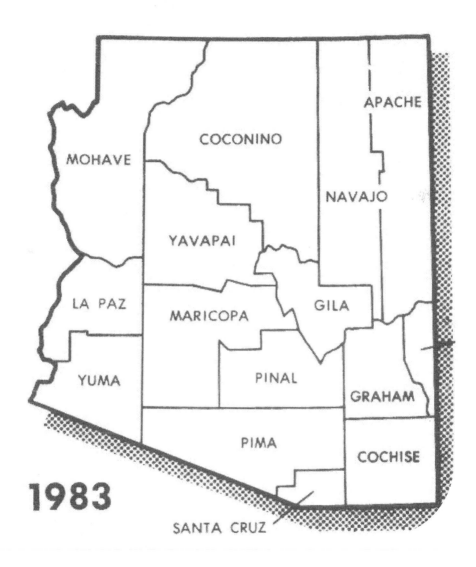

MIGHTY OAK CREEK

Two strong draws led to the initial settlement of the Sedona area. First, it was some of the last free land available under the Homestead Act of the 1860s. Second, and more important, Oak Creek, which runs through the area, is one of the few waterways in Arizona that runs all year long. If you were close enough to the Creek, you could irrigate and you could farm. Obviously, the land along the creek became the most desirable homestead acreage.

In 1876, Jim Thompson wandered down along Oak Creek and found a spot where corn, beans and squash were growing...a sure sign that farming could be successful. He squatted on the land, and then homesteaded, becoming the first Anglo to settle in Oak Creek. (A small band of Apache had been removed to a reservation a short time before.) Homesteads eventually sprung up along the creek as it found its way to the Verde River. Oak Creek split the areas of settlement; settlers and schools often on opposite sides of the creek.

The semi-arid Red Rock Country depended on the flow from Oak Creek. But Oak Creek has been and is fickle in her behavior. Low water crossings were critical to the homesteaders, especially along the loop area of the creek. The Owenby, Schuerman and, finally, the Baldwin families always made sure they could cross the creek. The location of the crossings changed from year to year, depending on the reconfiguring of the creek due to runoff. Where there was a shallow spot with good rock close to the surface would determine which family would be responsible for a crossing. More gravel and rock would be added allowing horses and wagons to move from one side of the creek to the other. Children from Big Park (originally called Eagle Valley by the Apache) went to school in Red Rock across the creek.

Where they crossed changed each year. Sometimes, if the runoff came while they were in school, they couldn't get home.

Floods were a fact of life. The Schuerman family was "flooded" out more than once. In 1938 an unusually heavy flood wiped out all the small low water crossings that had been in use. This led to the relocation of the crossing to the slippery rock at Baldwin's Crossing, now known as Red Rock Crossing. In 1978, Sedona and the Village of Oak Creek experienced two 100 year floods in one year, washing out the concrete low water bridge put in by cowboys years earlier. There were rock slides in Oak Creek Canyon, Mayhew's Lodge lost its footbridge, the wooden auto bridge at Indian Gardens broke loose, and Red Rock Crossing became victim to the flood. Quirky Oak Creek continued to have its way with man- to show who was boss. There have been floods since that year, just not quite as destructive. Man proposes, the creek disposes.

A CREEK CROSSING

Why do you cross a road? To get to the other side, of course. Why do you cross a creek? For the same reason: to get to the other side. And Oak Creek was no exception. There has been a crossing of sorts (low water) along the loop area of the creek ever since the area was first homesteaded. The Owenbys, the Schuermans, the Baldwins, etc. all took the responsibility to make sure they could get to the other side. One may assume that before the first homesteaders, the Indians who lived in the area had their own means of getting across the creek safely. Rumor has it that General Crook's troops built low water crossings to remove those same Indians from the area before the homesteaders arrived.

Every spring the crossing was in a different place. The heavy run-off reconfigured the creek and mandated that the "crossing" be redone every year. Wherever the creek was most shallow each spring, with good rock beneath the surface, would determine which homesteader would have the task of creating the primitive crossing. Gravel and rock were moved into a low area to make it a viable means of getting across Oak Creek for horses and wagons initially, for motor vehicles in later years. Because of the heavy run-off, the creek would be too deep for horses and wagons to cross anywhere without some help from the local farmers.

A low water crossing was a critical necessity from the late 1800s. It provided the quickest and safest route from Big Park to Red Rock--the original settlement in the area—and back again, and from there to Cottonwood. Red Rock is located about one mile northeast of the entrance 18 to today's Red Rock State Park. (The areas that would later bear the name Sedona were originally known as Grasshopper Flat and Lower Oak Creek.) Children from Big

Park went to school at the Red Rock schoolhouse, but they had to cross the creek to get there. If it ran too deep, they could not get to school. If the run-off came down during the day after the youngsters were in school, they couldn't get home. They then bedded down with folks in Red Rock or in the schoolhouse itself.

The crossing (wherever it happened to be that year) was used primarily by the Owenbys and the Schuermans. What is now called Red Rock Crossing, sometimes known as Crescent Moon Ranch, was eventually sold to Andrew Baldwin, and was officially designated as Baldwin's Crossing.

This worked just fine until the big flood in 1938 wiped out the small crossings that had been used up to that time. After the flood, the crossing was relocated to the slippery rock at Baldwin's Crossing. Boulders and gravel were trucked in to fill the crevasses in that rock, making it easier than ever to cross the creek. Yavapai County took authority over this route in the 1940s, laying a grid and filling in with cement. Oak Creek Crossing became a popular route to get from here (Big Park) to there (Red Rock). Popular route, of course, is a relative term. In the early 1950s, there were fewer than 100 families in the Sedona area. The low water crossing was not subject to much in the way of heavy traffic, even if it was the only way to cross the creek. Red Rock Crossing continued as a county road until the flood in the 1970s when it washed out completely. Quirky Oak Creek continued to have its way with man-made crossings to show who was boss. It just took a little longer this last time. Man proposes, the creek disposes.

Crescent Moon Ranch was sold by its last owner, Nick Duncan, to the Forest Service who developed Crescent

Moon Park. You can still cross the creek at Red Rock Crossing. Just make sure it's at low water because you'll do it by foot. (My thanks to Sherman Loy and to the Sedona Historical Society)

HAPPY BIRTHDAY, ARIZONA

Arizona has been a land of romance and a land of exploitation since it was first peopled more than 12,000 years ago. It was the land of the Pueblo civilization (the original "Village People"). The heyday of these ancient Pueblo People lasted about 500 years, from 700 A.D. to 1200 A.D.

Arizona was believed to be the location of the Seven Cities of Gold where streets were paved with gold plate and buildings were bejeweled. The king of Spain believed these tales and sent Francisco Coronado off to the New World to find these fabled cities and to bring back the gold. He was not as successful as the later "copper barons" who got rich on Arizona's mineral wealth.

The entire Southwest, including what is now Arizona and New Mexico, was acquired by the United States after the defeat of Mexico in the 1848 war. It was known as the New Mexico territory even though it was not an "official" territory. It was one huge blob of land between Texas and California.

The Federal government had been dragging its feet about making Arizona an official territory in its own right. There had been a heavy settlement of Southern sympathizers in the Tucson and Mesilla areas. Pre-Civil War Congress was loathe to give recognition to additional troublemakers. At one time the Washington folks had plans to bring both Arizona and New Mexico in as one huge territory, and later as one huge state. Sharlot Hall was one of the citizens who made sure that every legislator in Congress had a copy of the many objections to that idea.

In 1861, the people of Arizona (mostly around Tucson and Mesilla) passed an "Ordinance of Secession" and seceded from the Union. On February 14, 1862, the Territory of Arizona was recognized by the Confederate States of America as a Territory. This got the Feds moving, and on February 14, 1863, they recognized Arizona as an official U. S. territory, with the borders it now has. It was believed this would deter Johnny Reb from taking the southern route to the goldfields of California (whose citizens were more than a little sympathetic to the Confederate cause.)

In the 20th century, after much politicking, Arizona's constitutional convention included such novel reforms as initiative, referendum, woman suffrage, recall, and direct election of senators (not in the original U. S. Constitution). It led the rest of the country in many things. President Taft (whose dream it was to become a Supreme Court Judge) objected to the recall clause...it would allow the recall of judges. It was removed. The Arizona Convention had hoped Mr. Taft would sign the statehood bill on February 12, Lincoln's birthday. It was not to be. The President was in New York and would not sign the bill until February 14. (It seems Arizona was fated to have things happen on February 14.) Soon after the bill was signed, the recall clause was put back into the state constitution. Arizona women got the vote in 1912, eight years before the rest of the country. President Taft's dream came true. After being one of the few sitting presidents that was defeated in his re-election bid, he was named Chief Justice of the Supreme Court!

THE HAPPY WANDERER – OAK CREEK CANYON'S FIRST WHITE SETTLER

John James Thompson, one of the more colorful characters in Sedona's past, was born in Londonderry, Ireland in April, 1842. At the tender age of about 13, when today's youngsters are thinking about sports and make-believe adventures, John James (Johnny) ran away from his home and began a real life adventure that would take him half way across the world. This was near the culmination of the "great potato famine" in Ireland. Was he possibly orphaned? Or was he just rambunctious and a roamer at heart, even at that early age? Some say he ran away from religious persecution at home (his parents were strict Presbyterian). He made his way to Liverpool and tried to get a berth on a ship bound for New York. No responsible ticket agent would allow him to travel that far by himself. But Johnny obviously had a way with words (perhaps he had kissed the blarney stone). He convinced a young man who was about to sail on that ship to buy him a ticket and take him along as his kid brother!

When young Thompson docked in New York he met another youngster his own age whose father was a ship captain about to sail for Galveston, Texas. Johnny and his new friend thought it would be great fun to stow away and head for Texas to fight the Comanche. Alas, they were discovered two days into the trip and were put to work until the ship landed in Galveston. Johnny was allowed to go ashore where he wandered around alone in the strange city in the strange country. But the luck of the Irish held. Johnny got into a conversation with an old man named Finley. The man listened to Johnny's story, sympathized with his situation, and took him home to Refugio, Texas (just north of Corpus Christi) where he and his wife raised Johnny as their own. This is when "Johnny" became "Jim." There were three other boys who lived nearby by the name of John, so John James Thompson became Jim Thompson.

Jim grew up as a good Texan, and when Texas went "secesh," he joined the Confederate Army where he spent four years as a Rebel soldier. Part of the time he was in a prison camp in Illinois and part of the time he was in a hospital in Georgia recovering from a musket shot in his shoulder and arm.

After the war, Jim returned to Refugio, but the wanderlust returned with him. He headed down to Mexico, and four years later when he returned to Refugio, he took a job as a trail boss herding cattle to California. The crew, with Jim and his boss, left Texas in 1869, headed to Wyoming and then to Utah. Jim's boss sold the cattle in Utah, and everyone but Jim went back to Texas. Jim's wanderlust continued.

JJ Thompson and Family

Thompson followed rumors of a gold stampede at Diamond Creek on the Colorado in the Arizona Territory, and then down to Kanab Creek. Surprise, surprise, the rumors were just that...no gold. Jim was tireless and tenacious in his quest for adventure. He made his way down to the Virgin River where he began operating a ferry. In 1876, he sold the ferry, loaded up two wagons with pure rock salt from a cliff that was located near the ferry and headed to Prescott where he sold the salt. After an unsuccessful venture in the Mexican village of Phoenix, he headed back to Prescott where he sold his freight outfit, bought a saddle horse and pack mule, and headed for the Verde Valley. After farming for a year near Page Springs, Jim went exploring up Oak Creek in the canyon. He found Indian Gardens just a few weeks after the last Apaches were rounded up, was taken by the area, made a squatters' claim to the land and began to build a log cabin, the first white man to actually settle in the canyon.

It seemed that Jim was finally getting ready to settle down. He wrote to an old friend, Abraham James, extolling the splendor of Oak Creek Canyon. James came to the area with his family in 1878 and eventually settled on what became the Hart Ranch. Abraham had a daughter, Maggie, who was 22 years younger than Jim. But that didn't seem to be a hindrance to matrimony. They were married in 1880 when he was 38 and she was 16. Society sure would frown on that today. The Thompson/James match produced nine children, the last one born in 1911, six years before Jim's death in 1917.

The Thompsons lived in a cabin on what would become the George Jordan farm from 1880 until 1887 when they moved to Indian Gardens permanently. He built the first road from Indian Gardens to what is now Sedona, and in 1899 he helped establish the first school on upper Oak Creek. John James Thompson had finally settled down.

[Again, thanks to the Sedona Historical Society and to Albert Thompson's "How the Jim Thompson and Abraham James Families Came to Oak Creek"]

THE UNFORTUNATE MOUNTAIN MAN

Let me tell you a tale about a man who was tough as a nail. He feared no one and no thing. He was supremely confident that he could handle any situation that he met here in the hills of Oak Creek. You might say he suffered from a failing the ancient Greeks called "hubris"...excessive pride. And he paid the ultimate price. Richard Wilson was born and raised in Arkansas—folks weren't quite sure when, but he was "old" when he was hired by Jim Thompson in 1884 to help farm the Thompson claim up in Oak Creek Canyon. Dick Wilson had first wandered to Tucson, Arizona, in 1864, and eventually found his way (as wanderers in that time and territory seemed to do) to the canyon in Red Rock Country.

Jim Thompson had built another cabin down canyon, on what would become the George Jordan farm, to house his wife and children until he finished the cabin up in Indian Gardens. This was all still pretty wild country. In June of 1885, Jim had some business at the county seat in Prescott. (Remember, there was no Coconino County; it was all Yavapai County, which ran to the Utah border.) He was concerned about leaving his wife and small children alone while he was in Prescott for several days, so he asked Dick Wilson to come down from Indian Gardens every evening and spend the nights near Mrs. Thompson and the children. Wilson readily agreed.

Dick Wilson was excited about seeing the tracks of a "monstrous grizzly bear" between Sedona (called Camp Garden then, before the Schneblys came to the area) and Indian Gardens. He intended to get that big bear. Unfortunately, he had broken the sight from his bear gun and had only a small caliber rifle. Jim Thompson agreed to take the bear gun to Prescott for repair, but he made old Dick Wilson agree to leave the bear alone until Thompson returned. Wilson's intentions were good, but he was like an old war horse. He had bear hunting in his blood.

The very first evening Thompson left for Prescott Dick Wilson failed to appear at the Thompson cabin, as he failed to appear for the next seven days. Maggie Thompson couldn't go looking for him. She had a one-year old and a three-old, had no horse, and the nearest neighbor was five miles away. On the ninth day, John and Tom Goodwin, friends of the Thompsons, came by on their way up the canyon to do some fishing. Maggie voiced her concerns about Dick Wilson, she was sure something dreadful had happened to him. The Goodwins were not too worried, but assured her they keep a lookout for him on their way up the canyon. Sure enough, Maggie's instincts were right. The Goodwins were gone for only a short time before they came rushing back. They had found the old bear hunter's battered body a short way up the canyon, near the present location of Midgley Bridge. Poor Dick is dead, poor Dick is dead (my apologies to Rogers and Hammerstein).

At the inquest, they pieced out the story of what happened. Wilson had quit work early enough to get down to the Thompson cabin. He was on his way when he caught sight of the "old grizzly" and could not resist the temptation to get that bear. Despite the fact that he had only the small caliber rifle, he had no fear of the bear. He had spent a lifetime hunting and killing the critters. He shot the bear, but only wounded it. He then foolishly followed it up canyon where the bear turned and charged him. Wilson dropped his rifle, turned and ran for a tree, starting to climb it. The bear caught him by the foot before he got to safety, and pulled him down. His shoe showed bear tooth marks. The bear then either bit off part of Wilson's face or knocked it off with his paw, and then left. Wilson crawled to water puddle where he fainted face down in the puddle and drowned. Yes, indeed, poor Dick is dead.

Richard Wilson is buried at Indian Gardens. Fifteen years after the event, young Frank Thompson found the skeleton of a monstrous large bear near the top of what is now called Wilson Mountain. Folks agreed that indeed Richard Wilson had killed the bear even after the bear killed him. Both Wilson Canyon and Wilson Mountain are named after the bear hunting mountain man. Look to the west as you drive over Midgley Bridge and think a kind thought for the old grizzly hunter. [Again, many thanks to the Sedona Historical Society and to the wonderful memoirs of Albert Thompson]

BIG BEAR HOWARD

The saga of Jesse Jefferson (Bear) Howard reads like a western novel. He was born in 1817 in Illinois, and during the course of his long life he became the father-in-law, grandfather (and so on down the genealogy line) of the many Purtymuns who settled in Red Rock Country. He fought in the Mexican War under Sam Houston, was shot in the back and carried a bullet in his lung for more than 50 years. He married Nancy Cline and had two children — a son and a daughter--before she died in 1861. He was a big man, standing 6'8" in his stocking feet. Nobody messed with Jesse.

Howard was raising horses on a ranch in northern California in the 1870s. This was during the range wars between the cattlemen and sheepmen. There was a history of trouble between Howard and a Mexican neighbor who was grazing his sheep on Howard's land. He shot at the sheepman, intending only to scare him. Unfortunately, the sheepman died. Was Howard really that bad a shot? To his credit, he turned himself in to the law and spent several days in jail. The sheriff wasn't very sympathetic to sheepmen, so one night he left the jail door unlocked. Mattie, Jesse's daughter who was now married to Stephen Purtymun, was waiting with a horse. He was warned to stay away from California as he was now a wanted man. The Howard/Purtymun trek to Arizona began.

One of the first orders of business in Arizona was a name change. Jesse Jefferson Howard now became Charles Smith Howard. He found his refuge in Oak Creek Canyon. At that time he also changed his line of work. Whereas he had once raised horses, he now hunted and killed bear. He got so good in his profession that he earned the nickname "Bear." After a time, folks didn't remember his given name;

he was just "Bear." He took his kill up to a butcher shop in Flagstaff where they sold bear meat over the counter just like prime rib. Eventually, when the bear population diminished, he went back to raising horses.

Bear Howard became a legend in his own time. According to contemporary accounts at that time, the older he got, the stronger he got. Once, when he was being harassed by a particularly rough bunch of cowboys, Bear kicked up his foot from the floor and caught the ringleader under the chin, beat him in the face, peeling the skin back to his ears. It took 29 stitches to sew him back together. Bear was 67 at the time! The stories about him grew to mythic proportions. When he was 64 he married the widow Elizabeth James, a marriage that lasted 3 months. She didn't like his dogs or his tendency to give away her cattle to others.

Bear Howard died at the age of 93. His daughter, Martha Purtymun, was the mother of nine Purtymun children who would populate what we know as Sedona.

Photo of Bear and his cronies courtesy of:
Sedona Historical Society

OH – THOSE PURTYMUNS

The Purtymun name was synonymous with Oak Creek Canyon during the latter 19th century and early years of the 20th century. Martha (Mattie) Howard, the daughter of Bear Howard, married Stephen Purtymun in California before they found their way to Arizona. They had a passel of Purtymun children (nine of whom survived infancy) before she divorced Stephen in 1897. According to Mattie, Stephen had a drinking problem. He moved back to California and eventually Mattie married James Cook.

Purtymun Family
Photo courtesy of: Sedona Historical Society

There was a co-mingling of families. Cook had 5 children and Mattie still had most of her brood to rear. Unfortunately, Mattie didn't have much luck with husbands. According to family members, James Cook liked alcohol too well and was a notorious womanizer to boot. Divorce No. 2 was in the offing for Mattie. She continued to be productive and active for many years. Mattie was an exceptional seamstress and was noted for her quilts and knitting. She outlived both ex-husbands and four of her children.

Jess (or Jesse) Purtymun was the second son of Mattie and Stephen. He was born in California in 1879 and made the trek to Arizona with his parents and brother. Jess grew up and lived off and on for a time in a cave at Cave Springs in the Canyon. Later he farmed in the Canyon where he had about ten acres under cultivation. Like many of the early settlers, he was a man of several talents. Jess played the accordion for church services and for dances. He wrote songs and poetry. He did a little gold prospecting, and if rumors of the day be true, he also knew how to run a still.

Jess was a good-looking man…movie star handsome. (See photo) The ladies found him to be attractive — think a young Tom Selleck. He married Emma Arrowsmith and they had two sons. However, like the misfortune of his grandfather and his mother, this marriage ended in divorce. He then married Lizzie Thompson Nail, the eldest daughter of J. J. and Maggie Thompson. Lizzie had been married to Frank Nail. They had three daughters when Frank was killed on the railroad near Jerome. Lizzie and Jess had five children, four of whom survived infancy, Vera, Verna, Martha and Bud.

He worked for Coconino County for some time. He was part of the crew that built the road from the top of Oak

Creek Canyon to the city of Flagstaff while Lizzie and her daughter Myrtle cooked for the men. It was through the effort of Jess Purtymun that the first wagon road went through the Canyon. The county supervisors had promised that if the folks in Oak Creek would cut a road that could be driven over with an empty wagon, it would be made a county road to be maintained by Coconino County. It was done on July 3, 1914.

Jess died in February, 1941. Lizzie outlived him by 14 years. She died in March, 1956. They certainly left their mark in the Canyon's history.

ARIZONA'S WANNA BE BARON

Arizona has had some interesting folks in its past, some nutty folks, and some downright devious and dangerous folks. The would-be Baron of Arizona fits all the categories. He was one of the cleverest, most charismatic swindlers that graced this land of Arizona. Described by many of his contemporaries as a shyster, he certainly did his part to live up to that description.

James Addison Reavis was born in Missouri in May, 1843, the son of an itinerant business man and a half Spanish mother. Maria Reavis was extremely proud of her Spanish background and inculcated in James a grandiose expectation of his self-worth. From her he became fluent in Spanish. This would stand him in good stead in his machinations to own what would become Arizona. Prior to and during the Civil War Missouri was a hotbed of intrigue. At his mother's behest Reavis joined the Confederate Army, said Army being the one that held to the ideals of "Nobility, Chivalry, and the Glorious Past." However, the 18-year old soldier found that the romance of the army did not live up to his ideals.

Reavis did make an interesting discovery while in the army. He found he could forge his commanding officer's signature to get passes. When his fellow soldiers discovered what he was doing, he sold forged passes to them. When things were getting a little too warm, he took leave of the Johnny Rebs, surrendered to the Yankees, and eventually joined the Union Army. After the war, he made his way through various jobs in Missouri, finding outstanding success in forging and doctoring documents in land deals and real estate.

Reavis hooked up with George Willing, a physician turned prospector, and the two of them then became involved with William Gitt, an expert in Spanish land titles. Under the terms of the Gadsden Purchase and the Treaty of Guadalupe Hidalgo, the United States was bound to recognize and honor land grants made by the Spanish or Mexican governments. Lo and behold, Reavis had manufactured a fictional claim and then "acquired" documents supporting that claim to a Peralta land grant (about 18,600 sq. miles). Those documents found their way into records and archives supporting his claim. When there was still some question, Reavis married a much younger woman whom he claimed was the last survivor of the original Peralta line. She was actually a house maid that Reaves transformed into a Baroness (shades of Pygmalion). In the meantime he had convinced many of the very prominent men of business to confirm his claim. While the fraud was succeeding, Reavis collected about $146 million (in today's dollars) through the sale of quit claims, investment plans and rentals of mines! He even collected money from the Southern Pacific R.R. for right of way. He claimed that the pre-Columbian ruins at Casa Grande, AZ were part of the old Peralta hacienda.

The Baron got greedy. When an unfavorable Surveyor General report caused his claim to be dismissed, Reavis sued the United States for $11 million in damages ($304 million today). Early forensic investigation proved to be his downfall. Among other things, the inks used in the forged documents were not available in the centuries when those documents were supposedly written. The fraudulent 18th century documents were written with steel nibbed pens not used until the 19th century. He was tried and convicted of fraud and forgery, fined $5,000 (a pittance) and sentenced to 2 years in prison (he spent one year there). He died in Denver, CO in 1914 at the age of 71. There was never a dull moment in his life.

A DRIVE THROUGH OAK CREEK CANYON

In 1919, when young Henry Schuerman returned from World War I, he arrived in Flagstaff and was anxious to get back home to Red Rock along Oak Creek. Unfortunately, there was no easy way to get from there to here. His route home was a bit circuitous — from Flagstaff to Ashfork by train (53 miles), then south to Drake where he caught the narrow gauge rail through Sycamore Canyon to Clarkdale, then by motor car home with Major Midgely. A full day's travel time to get from there to here.

Nowadays, when my husband and I need a "canyon fix," we manufacture a reason to head for Flagstaff through 89A as it climbs through Oak Creek Canyon, a fifty minute drive to get from here (in the Village) to there. How and when did this wonderful road get built?

The first settlers in the Canyon had trails from near their properties up to the rim. They left wagons on the rim. When they needed to go into Flagstaff they would pack their horses and walk to the rim, hitch the horses to the wagons and ride into town. On the return trip, they would load the wagons, ride to the rim, unload the wagons and load the horses, and walk back down the trail to their homes. Prior to 1887, J. J. Thompson, the original settler in Oak Creek Canyon had built a primitive road along the creek bottom from Lower Oak Creek (present day Uptown Sedona) to his place in the Canyon (Indian Gardens). That road was washed out in one of the creek's many floods a few years later. J. J. and his sons spent the next several years building another road along the high side of the creek.

About 1900 Louis Thomas began work on a road from Flagstaff to his ranch on Oak Creek. The effort was underwritten by some Flagstaff citizens who liked to fish in Oak Creek, but did not like to use pack outfits to get to the creek. By the fall of 1906 the road was completed to the junction of West Fork and Oak Creek. Thomas could drive a wagon from his place to Flagstaff, but the eight miles between his place and Indian Gardens was a winding crooked trail that crossed the creek every few hundred yards. According to Albert Thompson, three miles an hour was top speed for anyone except the cowboys or expert horsemen. It was about then that Albert Purtyman came back to his ranch (present Junipine Resort) where he spent two years building a road the two miles between his place and the Thomas place. Starting in 1908, as the Howards, Pendleys, Purtymans and others settled or resettled in the area, they built roads that connected to each others' homes. The work was accomplished by strong backs, picks and shovels.

Jess Purtyman was instrumental in getting the first wagon road through the canyon. The Coconino County Supervisors had promised that if the people of Oak Creek could cut a road through the canyon that could be driven over with an empty wagon, it would be made a county road and be maintained by Coconino County. The settlers went at it. On July 3, 1914, the wooden bridge across the creek was completed at Oak Creek Falls (now known as Slide Rock) and the road between Flagstaff and the Verde Valley was open for travel.

When the road first opened, it crossed the creek 16 times between Sedona and the head of the canyon. Oak Creek, being what it was and is, flooded out several times in the course of the next few years. The 1918 flood washed out several of the crossings as well as the wooden bridge. In the spring of 1919, old Jess, with a county crew, rebuilt the road from Wilson Canyon to just below Indian Gardens. The first double lane segment of the road was built by the county in 1922. It extended from the crossing below Indian Gardens to Indian Gardens. During the 1920s, both Yavapai and Coconino Counties surveyed and planned, and then planned and surveyed even more to improve the road from Cottonwood to Flagstaff. (The Oak Creek Canyon section was dubbed "The Missing Link".) Finally, in March, 1929, the first contractor actually started work on the road from Sedona to Indian Gardens. Other contracts were let from 1931 through the mid-1930s. While work was being done in the canyon all traffic was stopped and diverted up Schnebley Hill Road. Midgley Bridge was finally built across Wilson Canyon. (The original Wilson Canyon bridge was behind the current Midgley Bridge.) This was the last major construction on the road. Contracts were let for paving the whole road, and when the paving was completed in 1939, the road was opened and taken over by the Arizona Department of Highways. A bit of trivia: originally known as State Route 79, the new "highway" officially became US 89 Alternate.

The next time you take that soul recharging drive up Oak Creek Canyon, take a moment to say thank you to those stubborn, hard-working folks who made it possible.

My thanks to the Sedona Historical Society and to Albert Thompson's Early Roads of Sedona Area

THE STAGECOACH WAS A'COMING

You've heard of the Deadwood Stage and the Butterfield Stage. But have you heard of the Beaver Head stage? It's not surprising if you haven't. It did not last long.

Did you ever notice the marker just off Highway 179 south of Big Park—near mile marker 302? It is an almost obscure recognition that there once was a station that provided mail service and transportation to the folks who lived in the Verde Valley. According to research done by Albert Thompson, little was written about the stage stop or the Star Mail Route that used the station. But in those early days, the only way to get to Flagstaff from the Valley was to leave from that Beaver Head stage stop, head up Woods Canyon by horse or mule, wander up a trail that is now I-17, make your way past Munds Park and eventually reach Flagstaff.

Research by Ellsworth Schnebly confirmed that the Star Line Transportation Company controlled the route from Prescott, Arizona to Santa Fe, New Mexico, eventually connecting with the railroad at Otero, New Mexico. The stage carried mail and passengers from Camp Verde, Beaver Head, Pine Springs, St. Joseph, eastward to Gallup and beyond. Martha Summerhayes (an Army wife), in 1875, described a torturous wagon trip bouncing over rocks from Fort Apache to Fort Whipple, by way of Beaver Head, where they camped out along the spring before the station was actually built. The stagecoaches made the first trip from Beaver Head to Prescott in 1876. Albert Thompson recalled that his mother talked about families heading to Beaver Head station to "fort up" when there were Indian scares. According to the newspaper, *Weekly Arizona Miner* (1879), passengers and mail could make the 500 mile trip from Prescott to Santa Fe in four days. It seems like 125 miles a day under primitive conditions was unbelievably fast. It could have been more hype than fact. Henry and Doretta Schuerman used this stage when, in 1884, they made their way from Prescott to settle at Red Rock via Camp Verde, Beaver Head and Big Park.

It is unclear when the stage stop was abandoned. General belief was that the mail route was discontinued when the Atlantic and Pacific Railroad was built across northern Arizona According to newspaper items from that time the mail and passenger line was beset with problems from Indians, crooked employees, and lack of money. The general consensus is that the stage stop was abandoned about 1882. The mail no longer came through, and folks from the Upper Verde and Upper Oak Creek had to go to either Prescott or Camp Verde for mail service. The stage stop was forgotten until the marker—giving little information--was erected in 1973.

A big thank you to the journals of Mr. Thompson and Mr. Schnebly

THE BIG SNOW

Martha and Sherman Loy during one of the later
snowstorms in the 1930s.
Photo courtesy Sedona Historical Society

Red Rock Country had one of its most spectacular snowstorms during the Christmas season of 1915. At that time of the year the annual Christmas program at the school in Sedona was the highlight of the season. It included Santa, a Christmas tree, food, gifts and dancing for all 35 pupils and their friends and relatives. After the party, everyone scattered to their homes, and the teacher, Edith Lamport, headed to her family home in Flagstaff.

The trip to Flagstaff was not a drive up 89A as it would be today. She went by horseback to Clarkdale where she boarded the train to Drake and Ashfork, from there to Flagstaff. Then it happened...a three day snowstorm that dropped 64 inches of the white stuff in the Flagstaff area, collapsing the movie theater in town. When the sky cleared, the temperature went down to 25 degrees below zero. The town came to a standstill. It took days before the Santa Fe Railroad was plowed out to begin running again.

It was time for Miss Lamport to return to her Sedona schoolhouse. She made her way via train back to Clarkdale. The storm that had dumped five feet of snow on Flagstaff was a little kinder to the Verde Valley. Red Rock Country had received a minimum of two feet throughout the area, with drifts several feet higher. Hay sheds and beams were smashed all over the Valley. The teacher made her way back to Sedona in stages. From Clarkdale she was taken to Cottonwood where she spent three days with Mrs. Willard trying to find a way into Sedona. An acquaintance named Worthington offered to take her by horse and buckboard the rest of the way. At Bridgeport (just east of Cottonwood) they lost sight of the road, and for safety's sake Worthington opted to head for the Hearst ranch in Cornville. After another three days, she made her way—on a borrowed horse—with the mail carrier, Wallace Willard into Sedona. After traveling twenty snow covered miles, they arrived that night to find a dance and party going on in the schoolhouse. Since no one had been able to travel since the storm, the hardy Sedona folks decided to make the best of it!

After seeing Miss Lamport home to Sedona, Mr. Willard still had to make his way to the post office, which was then located at Indian Gardens in Oak Creek Canyon. According to Albert Thompson, who was a boy at the time, the snow level up in the Canyon was more than three feet. Big tree limbs were broken by the heavy snow, blocking the road—such as it was. Willard wasn't sure exactly where he was going, but he trusted his mule to know the way. His trust was not misplaced. The mule was heading for food and rest, and he took his rider with him.

Although this Red Rock Country experienced a number of heavy snow falls over the years, in 1968 Thompson said that Christmas storm was the deepest in anyone's memory from the 1880s to the present time.

BLOODY BASIN

Like me you have probably driven back and forth to Phoenix, noticing the road sign along I-17 that says "Bloody Basin." Arizona is known for colorful place names, but this is a real winner! How in the world did a chunk of ground earn that gory nickname? Well, let me enlighten you. Bloody Basin is located in Yavapai County, along Bloody Basin Road, 23 miles east of Exit 259, which is south of Cordes Junction.

There are several myths that have sprung up regarding the naming of that piece of land. One of the most fanciful suggests that seven Navajo virgins were sacrificed at that spot by the Apache Geronimo to bring freedom to his own wives and children. Geronimo was a pretty savvy tactician (he kept the U. S. military chasing after him unsuccessfully for many years) and sacrificing young girls probably was not part of his game plan. And the myth describes "Navajo" girls who were indigenous to the northern part of the Territory while the Chiricahua Apache Geronimo's bailiwick was the southern part of the Territory and Mexico. Logically, it does not compute.

A second myth that makes a little more sense suggests that this land was pretty much cattle country. However, Basque sheepherders would drive their flocks to the area to graze, rotating between the valley and the mesa from the summer to winter. Now cattlemen did not appreciate this. Cows and horses eat foliage down to the ground so it will come back quickly, but sheep take the foliage down to the roots, which means nothing will grow back for several years. The cattlemen had enough and so they slaughtered all the flocks grazing in the area. The blood of the sheep covered the land, and hence...Bloody Basin. This was more probable since the Tewksbury (sheep)/Graham (cattle) Range War was covering much of the Tonto Basin (south of Payson) at the time. Close...but no cigar.

The real story, however, is a story of the battles between the military and the Tonto Apache. The Tonto were most feared by the Whites, who were looked upon as interlopers by the Indians. The Tonto-Apache were highly mobile and unpredictable—the same tactics used by their cousins the Chiricahua under Geronimo. They were scary.

In early March, 1873, a band of Tonto-Apache attacked and killed a party of three Whites, killing all three, but torturing one before he died. The atrocity spurred a punitive expedition under the specific command of Capt. George Randall, and the general command of General George Crook. The Apache were tracked to Turret Peak, a Yavapai stronghold in central Arizona. In late March of that year, Randall and a group of soldiers and scouts crept up Turret Peak at midnight. He had the men crawl to the crest on their hands and knees to be as stealthy as possible, not disturbing rocks or stones. At dawn they attacked. The Natives were so taken by surprise that they panicked, many of them jumping off the mountain precipice to certain death below. Those who resisted were quickly killed or surrendered. Estimates run between 26 and 57 Indians killed, with many more injured. No soldiers were killed. Several of them were later awarded the Medal of Honor. Two weeks after the battle many of the Indians surrendered to General Crook at Camp Verde and were removed down to the San Carlos Reservation, not to return until several decades later.

THE BURYING GROUNDS

What happened to the early settlers in Red Rock Country when they had completed their "allotted years" on earth? Until the 1970s there were few people here. Most who arrived after the1970s were buried "back home," close to families. Obviously that was not the case for the early pioneers. "Back home" was right here.

In pioneer days cemeteries were usually small family plots located on the farms or ranches. The first in the Red Rock area was located on the Schuerman ranch in the settlement of Red Rock. It lies about 4 miles from the intersection of 89A and the Upper Red Rock Loop Road, and within a mile of Red Rock Crossing. It was established in 1893 to provide a resting place for four year old Clara, daughter of Henry and Dorette Schuerman. Dorette later decided that there would be no Schuermans buried there because it was too close to their home. She spent many hours of many days at the site. From that time on Schuermans were buried in the Cottonwood Cemetery except for a still-born child of Henry Schuerman, Jr. who was buried there in 1932.

The cemetery, about a half-acre in size, is the final resting place for folks from Oak Creek Canyon, homesteaders from Big Park, and those who moved to winter quarters near the ranch so their children could attend Red Rock School. A few of the graves, outlined with rocks, mark the Mexican graves. A large weather worn wooden marker (completely illegible) indicates the grave of a Yaqui Indian who had worked as a scout with the army, chasing Apaches. Other familiar names marking gravesites include Thompsons, Purtymans, and Elmers. These were the folks who stayed and put down their roots in Red Rock Country.

Like the Schuerman Red Rock Cemetery, the Cooks Cedar Glade Cemetery, located next to the Elks building along Airport Road, was first located on a farm. The first burials occurred in 1918 during the Great Flu Epidemic. Henry Cook homesteaded the land in 1928, and he decided to create a permanent cemetery there since the graves were already in place. The first person to be buried there (in 1929) after the Cooks took ownership was Roene Wood, a three year old who had died of carbon monoxide poisoning during a truck trip from Cooks Hill to Munds Lake. Familiar names mark the graves in the one acre site. Sedona Schnebly and her husband, T.C., are buried there along with their five year old Pearl who had been killed in a riding accident in 1905. Originally Pearl had been buried on her family's land near Brewer Road and current Los Abrigados Resort, but was later moved to the Cooks Cedar Glade Cemetery. Some of the graves are unmarked, and some carry familiar names like Purtyman.

Cooks Cedar Glade Cemetery

Both cemeteries are now under the care of the Sedona Historical Society.

THE CAMELS CAME...AND WENT

A Bactrian (two-humped) Camel

If one day, when you are driving along I-40, you think you see a mirage that looks like a camel, it may not be a mirage, but the ghost of a camel from the U.S. Army's Camel Corps. Bizarre events were not unusual in the history of Arizona, however one of the most curious has to be the establishment of that branch of the military known as the Camel Corps.

With the Gadsden Purchase of southern Arizona in 1854, Secretary of War Jefferson Davis realized he had a problem both defending the harsh desert land and supplying the forts being built to defend it. Neither horses nor mules were up to providing the means of transportation. Davis (or an aide) came up with the idea of using the beasts of burden from the Arabian Desert, the Bactrian camel. Off went Major Henry Wayne to the Middle East with a $30,000 Congressional appropriation to purchase camels. He returned with 33 of the animals.

In 1857 the federal government was projecting to build a wagon road along the 35th parallel all the way from Santa Fe to California. Lt. Ned Beale of the Army Corps of

Topographical Engineers was chosen to lead the feasibility test. It was a perfect choice. The lieutenant was a colorful adventurer who was tenacious in successfully completing his mission. He was assisted by the camel caretaker, a happy go lucky Arab named Hadji Ali. It worked. In the summer of 1857, the group set out from Albuquerque with 23 camels, 350 sheep and 56 men. The Camel Corps successfully opened the wagon road that was the precursor of famed Route 66 and today's Interstate 40. This was the first federally funded road in the Southwest, costing the government $210,000.

The success of this mission prompted the federal government to cough up another appropriation, and 41 additional camels joined their kin in the American Southwest.

The camels did work for the army, and did roam the deserts not just in Arizona, but also California, Utah and Nevada. They were such reliable beasts of burden that more were imported for the military and for mining companies who used them in remote areas.

The advent of the Civil War ended the experiment. Some of the camels were sold, but many were abandoned and reverted to the wild state. However, they were never able to establish themselves and multiply in the wild. Settlers thought they were pests, and hunters decimated the population. The camels died out.

Down around Yuma, some of the old timers say a few camels—or their ghosts—are still out there. Some claim to have seen fresh camel tracks! And in Quartzite, ADOT built a tombstone for Hadji Ali (aka Hi Jolly), a pyramid of quartz and petrified wood topped by a tin camel.

Who knows? Maybe a ghost camel or two still travel along I-40.

THE CASNER SAGA

Casner Mountain, Casner Canyon, Casner Draw, and several other "Casner" place names. Who or what prompted such recognition here in the Verde Valley? That honor goes to a unique family by the name of Casner. Much of their story comes to us through the words of Rebecca Casner, the wife of Riley Casner.

Riley Casner was a widower with two children when he married Rebecca Frezell in California. She had been orphaned as a young child when her parents disappeared while looking for land on which to settle. Rebecca grew up and married Riley. They left California in a covered wagon and in 1875 settled near Jerome. Riley kept looking for the "right spot." For the next fourteen years, that right spot eluded them. They continued to live out of a wagon, along with several children (Rebecca gave birth to 12 children) and Riley's 100 year old mother, Jencie Jane. Rebecca cared for Jencie when she became an invalid until she died at age 104. Finally in 1889, their nomadic lifestyle ended. They moved to and homesteaded land near Beaver Creek. Their ranch is the present site of the Southwest Academy, southeast of the Village of Oak Creek.

They continued to live out of the wagon while Riley was establishing a reputation as a successful farmer and orchardist. The Casners slowly improved the homestead, eventually building a log house. But Rebecca continued to cook over a camp fire for several years. She used her egg and milk money to finally get a cook stove. However, Riley took it upon himself to trade Rebecca's cook stove for a horse he fancied! She never forgave him, although she again traded enough butter and milk to get another cook stove.

Rebecca's responsibilities didn't stop with the housework, sewing, preserving food, and raising their large family. Since Riley was "sickly," she also did most of the farm work, including the haying and the plowing. Rebecca outlived Riley. After his death she sold the ranch and moved to easier living in Camp Verde. She and Riley are buried in Middle Verde Cemetery.

Dan and Bill Casner were brothers to Riley. They arrived in the Verde area in the early 1870s. Dan and Bill were successful sheep men and often carried large sums of gold coins in their camps. One year when they were moving their sheep from Mormon Lake to Winslow they were both killed and the cache of gold coins disappeared.

Mose, another brother, was a colorful character. He and his mother (at a younger age) had run cattle near Sycamore Canyon and Casner Mountain. He later settled along Beaver Creek (currently Rancho Roca Roja). Mose was a miser, and stories about his wealth abounded. Supposedly he hid his gold coins in coffee cans and buried them in various spots. Legend has it that there is still Casner gold to be found in Sycamore Canyon and along Beaver Creek. When he was dying, he refused to tell anyone except his son where the gold was. His son arrived too late. There still may be gold in "them thar hills."

AN OLD TIME 4TH OF JULY

How did you all celebrate the Fourth of July in 2010? Here in the Village we had a golf cart and bicycle parade, games for all the kids, a water slide, and a picnic. Everybody was welcome. The folks in the early part of the twentieth century also believed in getting together to celebrate the birthday of this country. It was one of the four times in the year (Christmas, Easter, Fourth of July, and Thanksgiving) when the farmers and ranchers left their rather isolated spreads to meet, eat, gossip and have a good time.

The Fourth began with a bang...a really big bang. Early in the morning, someone (usually one of the Purtymuns) would light up a stick or two of dynamite, or possibly let off a volley of shotgun blasts. Guns would be shot on and off throughout the day, just for the fun of it. Families would travel via horse and wagon to a central meeting place. Early in the century the party would take place at what is now the Banjo Bill Campground up in the Canyon. Later the favorite meeting spot was Bacon Rind Park (still a favorite picnic ground). A dance was usually part of the festivities. Music held an important place in the life of the early pioneers. Many took it upon themselves to master the accordion, guitar, and especially the fiddle. If a fellow couldn't afford to buy an instrument, he used his creativity to build one. (A couple of "home made" instruments have been on display at the Sedona Heritage Museum.) Laura Purtymun McBride remembered that families would bring bedding with them so they could spend the night after dancing to the wee hours.

Food held a special place in the celebration. The Fourth was the time for a rare treat...home made ice cream. (Of course, there wasn't any other kind.) A day or so before the Fourth, one of the men would take a wagon up to

Flagstaff, pick up a 100 pound block of ice, cover it with canvas to keep it cool. After chipping and salting it, the ice was put into a wash tub. Ten gallon lard cans would be filled with the recipe and turned in the ice until ice cream resulted. Lemonade was another special treat. After the juice was squeezed into a large container, the peel was cut up and added to it along with water, sugar and some of the precious ice. Of course, some of the folks imbibed a dram of the stronger beverages that were available, courtesy of those creative pioneers.

According to Laura's memory, everyone would bring three or four different dishes. There were no hamburgers — or any kind of beef. There was no refrigeration, so the menu included chicken, ham, salt pork, beans, pies and cakes. Fresh fruit would be available.

Life was quite different in those days of yore. But they still managed to have fun with friends and family.

Old Time Fourth

ARIZONA – A CONTINUING CELEBRATION

Since the Centennial Year continues, let's recall some of the interesting and/or weird events from Arizona's past. Actually, this oddity is current today. Arizona is the only place in the United States where mail is delivered by mule. It's true...Supai village at the bottom of the Grand Canyon receives its mail by mule. According to Charlie Chamberlain—who was the "mail man" for well over 20 years—only mules (and maybe horses) could be depended upon to make the daily 3-hour one way trek to the bottom of the Canyon. The weather patterns over the Canyon are too "iffy" for dependable mail delivery by helicopter, and the mule train is cheaper. This mail does include UPS and FedEx, who, contrary to their commercials, do not deliver everywhere. Also included are all the hard goods and foodstuffs necessary to keep life going down at Phantom Ranch and Supai. The nearest supermarket is 100 miles away, so the mule train is really a life line.

An institution of yore, the University of Northern Arizona, has come a long way in just over a century. It came into existence as Northern Arizona Normal School on September 11, 1899, with 23 students, one professor, and two copies of Webster's International Dictionary. Four women made up the original graduating class in 1901 and were awarded lifetime teaching certificates for the Arizona Territory. For some years the school was a combination of high school and school for teachers until Flagstaff High School was built in 1923. According to Ellen Thompson Graves, after her father, Albert Thompson, completed the 9th grade in Sedona School, he moved to Flagstaff to live with his brother Fred so he could continue high school at the

Normal School. Albert graduated in 1912, the year Arizona became a state.

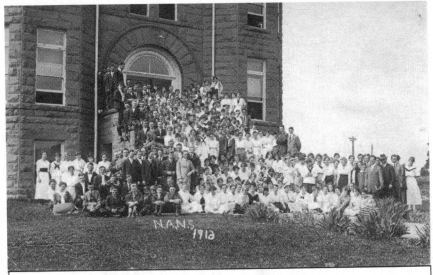

Northern Arizona Normal School Class of 1912
Photo courtesy Sedona Historical Society

In 1925 the school became Northern Arizona State Teachers College (and in 1929 Arizona State Teachers College) which could now grant the Bachelor of Education degree. In 1939, Ida Mae Fredericks became the first Hopi to receive a college degree. During WWII the student population dropped to a low of 161 students in 1944-45. With the end of the war and the addition of other degrees, i.e. Arts and Sciences, the name was changed again to Arizona State College. The returning war veterans swelled the student population. In 1968 the school became Northern Arizona University with the ability to award Doctorates. It had arrived!

A bit of trivia now. Karate was developed in Japan in 1936, but the first North American school of karate was opened in 1946 by Robert Trias in Phoenix. Mr. Trias is known as "the father of Karate in America."

ARMIJO HOMESTEAD/CROSS CREEK RANCH

When Juan Armijo homesteaded 320 acres near Oak Creek in 1892, he never dreamed that a century later his holdings would win a place on the Arizona Register of Historic Places. Thanks to the efforts of Jake Weber, local business man, the Armijo family and property will keep their place in the history of Red Rock Country.

The Arizona Register of Historic Places is the state's list of sites, buildings, structures and objects worthy of preservation. They are evaluated by the same criteria used by the federal government for the National Register of Historic Places. A property must be at least fifty years old. It must also be associated with historic events or activities; with an important historical person; have a distinctive design or physical character; or be able to provide important information about history or prehistory. The Armijo homestead met more than one of these factors.

Juan Armijo and his wife were both born in New Mexico. They came with their son Ambrosio to the Sedona area in 1892. Having been born in New Mexico, the Armijos were citizens of the United States and were eligible to file for land under the Homestead Act of 1862. In 1896, they filed on land that today is Cross Creek Ranch. At the same time they made arrangements to use and expand the irrigation ditch dug by Richard Huckaby, a neighboring homesteader. The ditch eventually became known as the "Historic Armijo Ditch."

In 1900 Juan posted claim for 160 acres along Oak Creek and claimed the right to 100 "miners inches" of water (a flow rate of about 2-1/2 cubic ft. per second) from the Creek to be used for irrigation. Also in 1900, Henry

Schuerman purchased the Huckaby property and then sold 80 acres of it to Armijo in 1906.

The Armijos farmed and raised cattle on the property for about ten years. They then rented out the land and moved to Holbrook. Shortly after his wife died in 1917, Juan married Yrene Peralta. He transferred the ranch to her before he died in 1921. She in turn deeded her share of the ranch to Ambrosio and, after settlement of his father's estate, he became the sole owner of the property.

Ambrosio moved back to the Armijo Ranch. He added a final parcel of land to the ranch in 1927, giving him complete control of the Armijo Ditch. This was significant. Irrigation ditches were of critical importance in the successful settlement of the area.

Over the next ten years Ambrosio added to the main ranch house, built a bunk house, barns and other outbuildings. He improved the Armijo Ditch with pipes, flumes and smaller ditches. In 1938, Ambrosio sold the property which included all the buildings, but more importantly, the Ditch with "all water and water rights…and the water flowing through the same" to a Los Angeles banker, Andrew Blackmore. The pioneer history came to a close. The cafe society history was about to begin.

ARMIJO HOMESTEAD TODAY

Armijo Homestead Today
Photo courtesy Sedona Historical Society

In 1938, when the old Armijo homestead along Oak Creek (near the present Red Rock State Park) was sold to Los Angeles banker Andrew Blackmore, its pioneer history ended. The property would change hands a number of times in the next seventy years. Blackmore kept the ranch only three years.

The next owners brought glamour to Red Rock Country. According to the records, Jack Frye, president of TWA, and his wife, Helen Varner Vanderbilt Frye (more about her later) were flying over the Sedona area in January of 1941. Helen fell in love with the country from up in the air. Six months later they bought the old Armijo ranch from Blackmore. Although they never made the ranch their permanent home, it became a vacation retreat. The Fryes were used to more lavish quarters than the simple ranch house, and they liked to entertain, so they remodeled the home to suit their personal lifestyle. Jack Frye was a close friend of Howard Hughes and often entertained him at the ranch. Others who spent time at the secluded retreat included Hollywood movers and shakers, federal politicians, and War Department bigwigs. Meetings sometimes included strategy sessions for the country's involvement in World War II. On a more romantic note, Elliott Roosevelt, son of FDR, and movie actress Faye Emerson honeymooned at the ranch after their 1944 marriage at the Grand Canyon.

In 1947, the Fryes sold part of the Armijo ranch to Albert Burhop for more money than they had spent for all their holdings along Oak Creek. The land they sold included the 140 acre core of what is now Cross Creek Ranch. The Fryes continued to buy and trade land until they owned more than 640 acres along Oak Creek. They called the property Smoke Trail Ranch. The house they built on the south side of the creek is known as the House of Apache Fires.

Helen and Jack divorced in 1950. She retained all the property along Oak Creek. During the 1950s she sold off pieces of the original Armijo ranch. They are now part of Cup of Gold Estates. In the 1970s Helen sold a 286 acre parcel of land—including part of the Armijo ranch—to a developer. This eventually became Red Rock State Park.

The Burhops kept their piece of the Armijo ranch until 1951 when they sold it to Willis Leenhouts, a teacher at Verde Valley School, who named the property Cross Creek Ranch. The Leenhouts raised sheep, built a pottery studio, and built a foot bridge across Oak Creek in order to access the property during high water episodes. In 1971 they sold the ranch to Harold Maloney, who planned to raise thoroughbreds. However, the Maloneys never lived at the ranch. A caretaker was hired to look after the horses and the property. The Maloneys acquired additional acreage to bring the total to 220 acres. In 2002, Cachet Homes bought the land from the Maloneys. The simple Armijo homestead had evolved into a state park, an upscale development, and a listing on the State Register of Historic Places. I wonder what Ambrosio would think about that.

Property history: courtesy Jake Weber

DOCTORING BACK THEN

What did the pioneers do when they had aches and pains and there was no corner drugstore, much less a doctor, nearby? They made do…with whatever was on hand.

What did the pioneer medicine chest hold? If you had colic or a sore throat you used ground roots and whiskey. Did your family have worms? Boil the bark of a peach tree and drink it for de-worming. Do you have a cut? And band-aids haven't been invented yet? Use kerosene or turpentine to hold it together, with flour, cobwebs and soot off the stove top to stop the bleeding. What would cure tonsillitis (hopefully)? Take 3 drops of kerosene on a teaspoon of sugar for three nights in a row.

The first doctor to actually practice civilian medicine was Dr. Myron Carrier who arrived in the area in 1881. Dr. Edward Palmer, attached to the army, did practice as a military physician in the late 1860s, but did not treat civilians. Dr. Carrier worked out of an office in Jerome, and made house calls in Oak Creek Canyon. His homestead was near Munds Park—he had married one of the Munds' daughters--and he actually served patients in Red Rock country while commuting between his office and his home!

The first dentist to practice in the area was Lee Hawkins. His office was in Jerome, and he owned and drove the first automobile there in about 1900. He was an amateur musician, as were many of the early settlers here. He also married Dr. Carrier's younger daughter.

Pregnancy and child-bearing were especially dangerous for women in early Sedona. Before there were doctors here, a woman either depended on mid-wives or actually moved to Jerome or Flagstaff during the last weeks of her pregnancy. This was the normal practice through the

1920s and 1930s. In fact, it wasn't until 1954 that Dr. Leo Schnur decided there were enough people in Sedona to support one physician. (Have you looked at the Yellow Pages in the recent phone book to count the number of doctors in the area now?) Schnur had been a doctor on the reservation and medical director of the Grand Canyon Hospital before he set up practice in Sedona. He operated the Oak Creek Medical & Dental Clinic until his retirement in 1969. His son, Paul, followed suit and had a plastic surgery practice until he moved to Scottsdale in 1988.

When one realizes that the importance of antiseptics was not realized until after the Civil War, that surgery to repair bone fractures didn't begin until 1870, and that the first successful appendectomy in the United States took place in 1887, it's amazing that the population of Red Rock Country actually grew over the years.

Dr. Carrier
Photo courtesy of Sedona Historical Society

DOUGLAS MANSION

Many tourists have been intrigued by the town of Jerome as it sits upon Cleopatra Hill. Most see and enjoy it as a charming little town that used to serve copper miners. The majority of visitors are satisfied by strolling through and spending money in the shops and restaurants that are part of Jerome's resurrection. But, if you are canny, you will find your way down to the Douglas Mansion also known as Jerome State Historic Park. It is an awesome museum with an intriguing past. If you have never been there, don't put it off. Go.

When the Douglas Mansion was built in 1916 Jerome was in one of its "boom" cycles. Traffic up Mingus Mountain was a nightmare. Everybody was heading for Jerome to get rich...or at least to find a job. The mansion was the grandest house in Jerome. In fact, it was one of the showplaces in all of Arizona. James Stuart Douglas, the owner of the Little Daisy mine, was used to style as well as comfort. He also wanted to impress his business friends and mining officials. Douglas was an interesting character. He was a Scotsman by heritage and had no problem saving pennies when it came to personal expenses (even wearing shabby, mended clothes), but he had no qualms about spending $150,000 (in 1916 dollars) for his hi tech mansion that had steam heat, electricity, and a central vacuum system that still works. He was most proud of the fact that the house was built of adobe bricks that were made on site.

Douglas was mindful of his employees. He built the Little Daisy Hotel as a dormitory for his miners. This was quite timely as his miners cut into an extremely rich vein of copper just as World War I created a huge demand for the metal and for men to mine it. The demand for copper increased even after the War. Arizona produced more copper than any other state. Copper production continued to escalate until 1929 when the big bust came. It wasn't only the Depression, but also low grade ore deposits that contributed to the bust.

Douglas' two sons chose different career paths from their father. Lewis chose politics, serving in the Arizona legislature, eventually going to England as Ambassador. James had a successful worldwide career in geology, but came back to work on the Little Daisy in its final days. The mine finally closed in 1938. The mansion was no longer needed as a residence.

The house stood vacant for a number of years while the family attempted to sell it. Our own "Belle of Bell Rock," Fannie Belle Gulick, who had amassed a fortune in Nevada mining as well as other enterprises, attempted to buy the mansion "to make the spacious house a haven for elderly prospectors and miners... for those no longer swinging picks and shovels." (Prescott Evening Courier, July 29, 1957) Unfortunately for the miners, these negotiations fell through and the mansion remained abandoned until the 1960s when the Douglas family donated it to the State of Arizona. It opened as a state park in 1965, and the succeeding years have been kind to it. And if you should happen to be near it after sunset, you just may run into a ghost from its past.

ARIZONA – A CONTINUING COMPENDIUM OF FUN FACTS

First of all, a commercial. In case you missed the early hoopla, the U. S. first class postage stamp celebrating Arizona's Centennial is a painting of our own Cathedral Rock. It really is one of the most attractive stamps commissioned by the federal government in recent years...and it's a "forever" stamp. If you buy them now, you can use them forever.

Photo courtesy Sedona Historical Society

Montezuma Castle, just south of Camp Verde, is Arizona's most impressive ancient housing community. Of course, Montezuma never came close to the area, but it is as close to a castle as could be found in this new world. Sitting up on the side of a huge limestone cliff, it is five stories high. Supposedly the Sinagua, who were traders and agriculturists, lived here and built the "castle" in the 12th century. It is mind-boggling to envision the tons of timber, rock and mortar that were carried up ladders to build those five stories, one atop another. By the mid 15th century the site was abandoned. Where did they all go? There are many theories, but the mystery remains.

Have you heard of the Mogollon Monster? According to various reports over the decades, it is at least 7 feet tall, covered in dark reddish-brown hair (except for the face), and leaves footprints almost two feet long. A foul stench surrounds it. Its stomping grounds range from Prescott to Williams to Winslow and around Payson. The first modern sighting supposedly occurred in the 1940s by cryptozoologist Don Davis when he was a boy scout. But, in 1903, the *Arizona Republican* reported that a tourist, I. W. Stevens, encountered a "wild man of the rocks" near the Grand Canyon. Is it possible that Arizona's Mogollon Monster is a cousin to Sasquatch or Big Foot? Arizona's Official Balladeer, Dolan Ellis, brought the Monster into an environmentally correct posture, by singing that the Monster ate only those children who litter!

Sunset Crater, merely twelve miles north of Flagstaff, was the result of a reluctant volcano. The underground rattled and shook until the pressure forced an eight mile long crack in the land, allowing steam, ash and liquid fire to burst to the surface, explode skyward, and fall back to the earth as cooled lava and dark cinder. This was not an unusual occurrence here in Arizona, land of many volcanoes. But most volcanoes of this type normally last less than a year. This one went on more than a century. According to the experts, at its end more than a billion tons of material covered the land. Ash, up to fifteen feet high, covered almost nine hundred square miles. The cinder cone was 1000 feet tall, a mile wide at its base, capped by a crater

400 feet deep. Wow! This treasure came under the protection of the Park Service in 1930, under Herbert Hoover, when Hollywood (a movie company) wanted to detonate the Crater to simulate an eruption. Arizona citizens were outraged, and, through their right of Referendum guaranteed by the Arizona State Constitution, petitioned for the preservation of Sunset Crater as a National Monument. It worked!

WHAT AND WHERE IS ELMERSVILLE?

I would guess that most of you have no idea what Elmersville is…or where it is. Would it help to know that as recently as 2006 the British folk music group "Callaghan" wrote a song and recorded a CD "Road to Elmersville" in honor of the settlement? Probably not. Well, you may be surprised to find out that Elmersville (sometimes called Elmerville) is our almost next door neighbor. It is located west of Lower Red Rock Loop Road, approximately 1 mile south of SR 89A. It is two miles west of the main entrance to Red Rock State Park. 'Map. Google.com' describes it as being in the Village of Oak Creek, but that's stretching it quite a bit.

Elmersville was first homesteaded in 1928 by Jesse James Elmer and his wife Jessie. At that time the area was called Jackass Flat. Back then the original dirt road near the homestead (89A) was the only road between Sedona and Cottonwood. In 1935 it became a two lane road, and today it is a 4-lane divided highway. In 1930 when the Elmers built their home there was no water on the property. They had to haul water from Oak Creek almost a mile away. Can you imagine — barrels loaded on a trailer backed into the creek, and then filling those barrels with hand buckets! This was the only water they had for drinking, cooking, and washing clothes as well as bathing.

The Elmers had three boys, James Edward born in 1921, Jay William born in 1923, and Justin Leonard, born in 1937. Over the years the Elmer family made ends meet by ranching, orcharding, working a gas station in Clarkdale, and even taking extra roles in the many movies being filmed here in Hollywood East (otherwise known as Sedona).

The oldest boy, James, became a Marine and eventually settled in Chicago where he married Antoinette and raised a family of seven. The family moved back after his retirement in 1982. Second son Jay stayed in the area, working for the Phoenix Cement Plant. He and his wife Dorothy (who managed the Cornet Store in Sedona – remember that?) had 14 children. The youngest son, Justin, married Carol and stayed in the area. That's a heap of Elmers in the settlement of Elmersville.

For a lot of years the settlement was populated pretty much by members of the Elmer family. In the last twenty or so years, emigrants from big city life, overcome by Red Rock Fever, have discovered the serenity of the Elmersville area. Do the names Cross Creek Ranch, Cup of Gold, and Eagle Mountain Ranch sound familiar? They are all close neighbors of Elmersville.

The road was officially named Elmersville by the electric company. But when Yavapai County got around to putting up a street sign a few years ago, they misspelled the name and called it Elmerville. And now you know where it is.

Thanks to Betty Cook and to the Sedona Historical Society

FARMING AND RANCHING

There were two main reasons why this part of Arizona was settled. It was some of the last free land available under the Homestead Act of the 1860s. More important, Oak Creek is one of the few waterways in Arizona that runs all year long. Farming in the area was successful only if water was available. If you could irrigate, you could farm. The early settlers—Thompsons, Jameses, Purtymuns, etc.—all homesteaded near Oak Creek. They may have been flooded out occasionally, but water was close by to easily irrigate their small farms.

When the Jordan brothers planted their orchards in the late 1920s and early 1930s, they used the technology available to successfully bring crops to fruition. George's orchard was close to Oak Creek, near the present day Art Center. Simple irrigation methods worked for him. Walter's orchard was planted in what was called dry land or a dry farm, not close to the Creek. Fortunately, the brothers worked together. George was an engineer, and with Walter, he developed a method of bringing water up from the Creek through a hydraulic pump system, storing it in a natural sink just above the Walter Jordan property, and irrigating the fields during dry spells.

As an interesting side note-- since it takes at least four years for an apple tree to produce fruit, Walter Jordan earned a living by growing CARROTS! He then huckstered them to hotels and restaurants in Phoenix, including the famous Westward Ho.

Henry Schuerman was successful in planting an orchard and a vineyard near Red Rock because his land was located on Oak Creek near Big Park (present day Village of Oak Creek).

Grasshopper Flats (West Sedona) was considered to be pretty much a waste land not suitable for farming or settlement because it was too far away from dependable water, i.e. Oak Creek. In the late 1940s Fanny Belle Gulick, who had acquired the land a few years earlier, hired a well driller, Carl Williams, to sink a well in the area. Lo and behold! Water and plenty of it. West Sedona was on its way.

Ranching was always a way of life in the area, beginning with the early settlers. But no one got rich doing it. According to the old timers it took 50 acres to feed one unit—a cow and a calf. The ranchers wintered their herds here in the Oak Creek/Big Park area where the weather was milder. Come springtime, the herds were moved up through Jacks Canyon, the Schnebly Hill area, or the canyons north of Sedona, eventually finding pasture near Munds Park and Flagstaff. The grasses provided lush fodder for the animals. According to Sherman Loy, in one of his off the cuff discussions, there was no big problem with forest fires back then because the cattle ate all the low lying shrubs and grasses that provide the "tinder" that feeds Arizona's fires today. It was the natural order of things.

Jordan Waterwheel

FORT VERDE – HOW IT CAME TO BE

Old headquarters for the fort, used for admn. and commander offices. Was used as first Indian School in AZ after army left, then a post office.

Photo is at least 100 yrs. old.
Photo Courtesy Sedona Historical Society

Most of us have made a trip or two down to Camp Verde for the Pecan and Wine Festival, the Corn Fest, or a bit of gambling at the casino. But have we ever wondered how and why Fort/Camp Verde came to be? Let me enlighten you.

The Verde Valley was inhabited off and on by native peoples for centuries. By 1860 there were folks living in the valley again. However, the indigenous people were being besieged by immigrants moving into the rich, arable area near the Verde River, those immigrants grabbing land and killing wild game. The original inhabitants (the Yavapai and the Tonto Apache) fought back against the immigrants (the Anglo Americans) by raiding their crops and livestock. But the immigrants had "might" on their side. They appealed to the government for help. Arizona had finally become a Federal territory — only after Jefferson Davis had declared it a Confederate territory — in 1863. So the demand for help was heeded.

A volunteer military unit was dispatched from New Mexico. In 1865 they built a tent camp along the Verde River called Camp Lincoln about 5 miles south of present Camp Verde. By 1866 (the Civil War had ended and troops were available) the Regular Army relieved the volunteers. They used this site from 1866 to 1871. In 1868 the name of Camp Lincoln was changed to Camp Verde. The site of Camp Verde was afflicted by malaria and a decision was made to move the Camp. Between 1871 and 1873 there were 22 buildings and a parade ground completed at the present site. In 1879 the name of the camp was changed to Fort Verde to establish its permanence. Like most of the forts in the Southwest, there was never a wall or stockade around the buildings. And there were never any actual battles at the Fort. It was used as a staging area for military projects, i.e. a wagon road from Fort Whipple (near Prescott) southeast to Fort Apache. But its primary purpose was to keep the Indians under control through the Reservation system.

The Rio Verde Reservation, established in 1873, was headquartered near Cottonwood. Nearly 1500 Indians were settled on the 800 square mile reservation. They had built an irrigation ditch with help from the military and had about 60 acres under cultivation. Things seemed to be going well until some malcontent businessmen from Tucson, who had some clout with the U.S. Congress, demanded the removal of the Indians. In late February of 1875 another "March of Tears" began. The Indians were removed to San Carlos. More than 100 of them died from exposure and hunger. Their reservation was opened to settlers and miners in 1877.

Meanwhile, Camp Verde became much less important. By 1891 it was officially abandoned. The military base was gone, but the settlers who made the area their home remained. In 1899 small parcels of the base were sold off at public auction. In the 1950s Camp Verde citizens banded together to preserve the old military fort as living history and a museum. The buildings and ten acres now sit in the center of Camp Verde as a state park.

THE RED ROCK WINEMAKER

Meet Henry Schuerman, a gentleman who played a major role in the settlement and growth of Red Rock country.

Heinrich was born in Germany in 1852. He was a baker by trade. Europe was in turmoil during that period, and in Germany young men were being conscripted to fight in the continental wars. Seventeen year old Heinrich opted for something else. He left Germany and made his way to Canada, and then the United States. For the next ten years he worked his way through this country, earning his living as a baker. He eventually headed west, ending up in Prescott, Arizona.

In Prescott, Heinrich and a cousin ran the old Pioneer Hotel until 1884. But Heinrich (now Henry) was getting lonely. He wanted a family and real roots. Over the years he had kept in touch with his childhood friend, Dorette Titgemeyer. She was still unmarried at age 29 — did not want to be an old maid--and was amenable to Henry's proposal to emigrate and to marry him. Henry met Dorette in New York City where they were married in June, 1884.

In 1882, Henry had taken deed to farmland on Oak Creek in payment of a $500 debt. In 1885, Henry and Dorette traveled to Red Rock Country to look at the farm. After five days of travel from Prescott to Big Park, and finally across Oak Creek, they reached what would become the settlement of Red Rock (near Red Rock Crossing). They had no intention of staying, but they could not give the land away, much less sell it. They didn't know what else to do so they settled in. They were not farmers, but they planted crops, including zinfandel grape vines. Henry had a knack for wine-making. They built a home, irrigation ditches, and roads to market the eventual abundance of fruits, vegetables, and especially wine.

They became prosperous. Henry was very successful with the vineyard. He built a winery known as Red Rock Grape Wine. When the mines opened in Jerome, he had a steady stream of customers. He built a schoolhouse, donating both land and money, because education was a high priority with Henry.

The Schuermans survived more than their share of troubles. They had to re-purchase the land they couldn't give away. It was actually owned by the railroad who did sell it back to Henry. A child died, homes either burned to the ground or were washed away by an Oak Creek flood.

In 1915 Arizona passed a prohibition law (five years before the rest of the country), so Henry's trade made him a lawbreaker. He spent some time in jail for illegal winemaking, later being pardoned. But his health deteriorated. The stress of his problems caught up with him. Henry died in 1920, leaving quite a legacy here in Red Rock Country.

OUR HISPANIC PIONEERS

When we think of the early settlers of Red Rock Country, the names Thompson, Purtyman and Schuerman quickly come to mind. There are other names not so familiar that deserve recognition: Chavez, Armijo and Nuanez.

Manuel Chavez, a former army scout from the Apache campaigns, moved from Flagstaff to the area near the settlement of Red Rock. He traded an old wagon and a set of chain harness for squatters' rights to a ranch just north of Red Rock Crossing. Mr. Chavez filed on the ranch and went about improving it to gain title. (The Doodlebug Ranch, near present day Poco Diablo, was part of the original homestead.) At age 70, he had not been able to secure the army pension to which he was entitled. He rode horseback alone from Sedona to St. John's, Arizona, where he hired an attorney who helped win his pension. His son, Ambrosio, completed filing on the ranch and successfully raised cattle and vegetables which he sold in Flagstaff and Jerome. The road to the Chavez ranch was once called the "Old Mail Route" because it was the only road to Flagstaff before Munds Trail and Hwy. 89A were built. Chavez Crossing, a ford across Oak Creek leading to the road, memorializes the Chavez name.

Juan Armijo, a friend of Manuel Chavez, actually came to Oak Creek and filed on a homestead three years before his friend came to the area. He and his son settled on two parcels totaling about 350 acres. Some of that land is now Red Rock State Park and Cross Creek Ranch. The ditch he built is known as the "Historic Armijo Ditch." Juan took title to his land in 1913, but his son did not complete ownership of his homestead until 1939. Mr. Armijo served as Justice of Peace for the Red Rock District. Juan Armijo's son married a daughter of Manuel Chavez, thus cementing a family relationship between the two prominent Hispanic families in the area.

Juan Nuanez, another son-in-law of Manuel Chavez, tried to file homesteading papers on 80 acres near Back O'Beyond. However, there was some question about his citizenship and Mr. Chavez took over the claim. When the citizenship question was eventually cleared up around 1908, Mr. Nuanez was able to claim acreage in the same area. He "proved" the claim in 1920.

Another Nuanez family member was Letatio, better known as Al. He was born in Jerome in 1909, but spent his early years on a homestead near Back O'Beyond. He was orphaned by age nine and eventually went to live with his uncle Ambrosio Chavez on the Chavez Ranch. He helped build the landmark house on the Doodlebug Ranch. Al grew up around horses and cattle. This led to his career as a stunt man and extra in the movie industry. His first movie as a young man was "Riders of the Purple Sage" and his last movie at age 75 was "The Return of the Killer." This was filmed in Sedona in Spanish for distribution in Mexico.

These Hispanic pioneers were certainly significant players in the Sedona saga.

THE JORDAN ORCHARD

In 1930, Walter Jordan and Ruth, his college educated wife from the Phoenix area, began planting the acreage in north Sedona (at the end of what is now Jordan Road in Uptown) that Walter had acquired from his father, Will. Eventually this would become the Jordan Orchard. In 1931, he built on the property the one room cabin which became the nucleus of the farmstead. Walter's plan was for an orchard, but until the apple and peach trees would start producing, the Jordans supported themselves with carrots, beans and strawberries.

Jordan Orchard
Photo Courtesy of Sedona Historical Society

Walter and Ruth lived in the single room and begat three children: Annie in 1933, Ruthie in 1934 and Walter, Jr. in 1937. It wasn't until 1937/38 that the first addition to the house was made (through the generosity of his mother-in-law so she could spend summers away from Phoenix). Two bedrooms and a bathroom with running water and a flush toilet. That was pretty fancy living in those days...anywhere in rural America, especially end of nowhere Sedona. Now Walter was well on his way to becoming the crusty, cantankerous old curmudgeon that he did, indeed, become. If his mother-in-law was willing to spend her money to enlarge his house — well, God bless her. She died just a year and a half later having enjoyed the cooler summers for a very short time!

The rest of the house was built in 1947, after World War II. You can believe that Ruth thought she was in heaven, going from the one room cabin in 1931 to just over 3,000 square feet in 1947. Only the one family — the Walter Jordans — lived in the home. As the business prospered, the home expanded. It was in the 1970s, as Walter and Ruth were aging, that they began selling off the land. The children were not interested in trying to keep the family orchard going, and had, in fact, moved from the area. Annie and Ruthie moved to the metro Phoenix area, and Walter, Jr. moved to Pennsylvania. Walter died in 1987. Ruth Jordan lived in the home for a number of years after Walter's death, but when it became obvious that, even with help, she could not stay at the farmstead, she sold the house and remaining acreage to the city of Sedona. She moved to an assisted living facility, and died there in the mid-nineties.

The city and the Sedona Historical Society became partners in a venture that would become the Sedona Heritage Museum. It was an opportunity to offer its citizens a link to the area's history and to offer tourists (Sedona's biggest industry) something other than tee shirt shops and galleries filled with art that few people can afford. It was a chance to show the real history of the west as it was not too long ago.

The home and outbuildings are on the National Register. If you haven't been to the Museum you really should come and take a look at a way of life that is fast disappearing. It is a gem in Sedona's jewel case.

FARMSTEAD TO HERITAGE MUSEUM

How does an Arizona farmhouse become a respected Heritage Museum? It begins in 1880 when the Wil Jordan family came into the Verde Valley. Wil and Annie (Bristow) Jordan had a passel of kids, Walter and George being Nos. 6 and 7. The Bristows and Jordans were orchardists. They and several others had planted orchards in Clarkdale along the river; those orchards were severely damaged and ultimately ruined by sulfuric smelter smoke. Wil then bought land in Bridgeport, hoping that would be far enough away, and safe. Unfortunately, the company built a new smelter in Clemenceau (Cottonwood), and it was the same smelter smoke story! This time the farmers fought back and sued Phelps Dodge for damages. Eventually they did win their suit.

In the meantime, Walter and George acquired land in Sedona at the base of Oak Creek Canyon along what is now 89A and uphill from that along Mormon Creek. They set about, separately, planting orchards. They combined their talents to build a water wheel, water pumping station, and irrigation systems that were a really high technology here in the high desert.

In 1930 Walter married Ruth Woolf, a teacher at Beaver Creek School. In 1931 they began construction of the one room cabin that would become the nucleus of the Jordan farmstead. They lived in that cabin and had three children. Walter planted peach and apple trees, but mostly apple. Until the trees were able to produce fruit, the Jordans raised carrots and other "truck farm" vegetables that were sold to restaurants and hotels throughout the state.

By 1938 their business was flourishing enough that they added two bedrooms and a bathroom with running water and a flush toilet. That was the height of luxury anywhere in rural America at that time, much less here in the boonies. It didn't hurt that his mother-in-law in Phoenix paid much of the cost of the addition so that she would have a cooler place to spend summers.

The orchard business became very successful. Jordan apples were sold not just in Arizona, but throughout the country. During WWII Jordan apples were shipped to GIs in Europe. As the business prospered, the house expanded. In 1947-48 the house grew to its present size, just over 3000 sq. ft.

Jordan Homestead

By the early 1970s the Jordans started selling off some of the acreage. They were getting old and their children were not farmers The Jordans continued to live here until Walter's death in 1987. Ruth stayed until it became apparent that she could not continue to live at the farm. In the early 1990s she sold the remaining property (about 4 acres) to the City of Sedona and retired to assisted living. She died in 1996.

The city and the Sedona Historical Society became partners in the venture that eventually became the Sedona Heritage Museum. It includes the farmstead and 3 outlying buildings, all of which are on the National Register of Historic Places. The Heritage Museum offers its citizens and the many tourists from all over the world a link to the American West the way it was...not so long ago.

HOUSE MOUNTAIN

Photo by Dave Benore

Standing guardian at the south end of the Village of Oak Creek and Big Park is an archaic remnant of the geological history of Red Rock country. House Mountain has its beginning at SR179 and hunkers westward to Page Springs, a distance of about seven miles. From Oak Creek on the north to Beaver Head Flats Road on the south it measures another seven miles. Although irregular in shape, it stills covers approximately 37 square miles. Quite a chunk of ground! Most folks driving along the Flats Road heading on to Cornville and Cottonwood are unaware they are passing along the remainder of a volcano that was active here after the area was an ancient sea. Over millions of years mountains thrust up, eroded away, seas formed and disappeared---while the continents collided and broke apart. Only recently has there been much interest in archeology and geology specific to Red Rock Country.

Sedona and Big Park not only straddle two county lines—Yavapai and Coconino, they also straddle two geological provinces—the Colorado Plateau and the Transition Zone (transitioning from the high plateau country in the north to Basin and Range country in the south). Its red rocks are related to the rocks of the Mogollon Rim.

Why are the rocks red? There is a thin coating of iron oxide (rust) on the outside of each individual grain of sand that makes up the rocks.

What about the volcano we call House Mountain? Most people would be amazed to learn that we here in the Village are living on the slope of a volcano. It isn't a dramatically erupting mountain like Mt. Fuji, but is rather a shield volcano. Shield volcanoes ooze very fluid lava for many miles in all directions when they erupt. Some academics disagree and believe it is the remnant of a free standing cone. Intensive study of this mountain began only in the 1980s. At first, it was believed to be about 5.5 million years old. But the mountain held a little mystery that belied this. More investigation revealed that House Mountain volcano lay beneath the ancestral Mogollon Rim. Lava flowed only to the east, south, and west. The Rim blocked any lava flow to the north. As the Rim receded to its present location (it's still receding at the rate of one foot every 625 years) Big Park was formed. Based on this information, it is estimated that House Mountain is about 14.5 million years old and is resting quietly.

Native American people called the mountain Big Eagle Mountain, and Big Park was called Big Eagle Valley. (If this area ever incorporates, Eagle Valley might be the least divisive name for it.) Mrs. David Dumas is given credit for naming this mountain because she saw on its top a basalt structure that resembled a house, with a taller structure that seemed to be a chimney. Lightning later destroyed the chimney.

So take a look at House Mountain and appreciate it for what it is...a link to the ancient past.

APPLES--SEDONA'S FIRST INDUSTRY

It is no secret that farming in Arizona is successful only if water is available.

Oak Creek, as it flows down through the canyon to meet the Verde River, provides the resource that allowed the first successful commercial endeavor in Sedona.

In 1930, before Rt. 89A was completed through the canyon, Walter and George Jordan acquired land in what is now Uptown Sedona. George had about 175 acres near Oak Creek (the Sedona Art Center now sits on the land) and Walter owned about 110 acres of dry land farm uphill from George's place (now the site of the Sedona Heritage Museum). The brothers worked together to plant most of the acreage in apples, with some in peaches. It takes about eight years before the trees mature to become commercially productive, so truck farming provided for their livelihood.

George's orchard was close enough to the creek for a simple irrigation ditch with a hydraulic ram driven pump; however, Walter's orchard provided a bit of a problem. It was dry and it was up hill. Walter was an orchardist, but George was an engineer as well as an orchardist. He designed and the brothers installed a turbine generator in Oak Creek which operated an overshot water wheel, 20 feet in diameter, that pumped water through piping to a reservoir up hill to the west of Walter's farm. The orchards were then gravity fed from the reservoir.

The Jordans produced high quality fruit and vegetables. Their customers were not limited to the Verde Valley, but included Flagstaff and Phoenix. During World War II, Walter contracted with the U.S. Army to ship 1000 boxes of apples to Phoenix in one week. Since I-17 did not exist, the route went from Uptown Sedona to Jerome, over

Mingus Mountain to Prescott, through Wickenburg to Phoenix, 12 hours down loaded and 8 hours back empty.

New markets opened and increased production demanded mechanization. Walter built a packing shed in 1946 to house what was then a state-of-the-art grading machine. Before installation of the machine, local residents (there weren't very many in those years) sorted, graded, and polished the apples by hand. They sat on boxes and wore gloves to polish the fruit. Although this had been a pretty primitive "assembly line," it had provided the locals an opportunity to make cash money for their labor, a basis for economic stability.

The grading machine did away with the drudgery of hand labor. The fruit was automatically sorted by weight and polished with horse hair brushes. It stayed in operation until the Jordans retired from the business in 1972. They were getting old and tired, hired help was hard to find, and by the 1970s refrigerated tractor trailers were hauling produce across the country on interstate highways. Additionally, there was no way to compete with the corporate farms coming into being at that time. But from 1930 to 1970, the Jordan Apple Orchards were a major factor in the growing economic stability of this Red Rock haven called Sedona.

WILL AND ANNIE JORDAN

The name "Jordan" is an integral part of Sedona's history. Brothers Walter and George Jordan, through their orchards and dry land farming technology, created the commercial operation that (along with the movie business) would allow the economy of Sedona to flourish. The Jordans came from good, tough stock. Their father, Willie Albion Jordan, born in 1859, moved from Cape Elizabeth, Maine, to the Upper Verde area in 1880...possibly in response to Horace Greeley's injunction to "Go west, young man." He was 21 at the time. In 1886 Will began farming 80 acres on the Upper Verde (Clarkdale). In 1889 he met and married Annie Bristow. Their marriage produced nine children.

Annie T. Bristow, born in 1869, came to the Arizona Territory at the age of six after a four month journey by covered wagon from Missouri to the Middle Verde area. Her father, Parson James Caulson Bristow, was the first ordained Baptist minister to come to this area.

By 1911, Will began acquiring additional farm property, with the Bridgeport farm being purchased in 1912. He had sold part of the Clarkdale farm to William Clark who then built a smelter to refine ore from the Jerome mine (see photo). By 1919, the Jordans, along with 12 other farmers, filed suit against the United Verde Company for crop damage caused by sulfur smoke from the smelter. (So you see – pollution was not a problem unique to the late 20th century.) The suit was eventually successful (it went all the way up to the Federal Supreme Court), and they were paid for their losses in 1924. In 1926 the settlement money was used to purchase the Sedona property. Will and Annie never actually lived on the Sedona property, but stayed on the Sugar Loaf Ranch in Bridgeport, although Will, Walter and George farmed the property, producing quality fruits and vegetables.

Much of present Uptown Sedona is part of the original purchase of 175 acres. In the 1920s Will traded 12 of those acres on Oak Creek to Jess Purtyman for 65 acres of dry farm property — the Sedona Heritage Museum now sits on part of those 65 acres. This property was originally acquired by Frank Thompson in 1914, and then traded to Jess Purtyman who traded and sold the land to the Jordans (real estate transactions were both casual and complicated back then). Walter was a farmer and orchardist, while George was an engineer and an orchardist, a rewarding blend of skills. The Jordan men successfully farmed those acres that today encompass Jordan Historical Park.

Will Jordan died in 1952. Annie Jordan died in 1957.

Will and Ann Jordan with Family
Photo courtesy of Sedona Historical Society

JOURNEY TO JEROME

Many of us have traveled up Mingus Mountain to enjoy the quaint little town of Jerome. We have wandered through funky little shops, enjoyed its wonderful museums, dined in its delightful restaurants, and been intrigued by the ghosts who walk through the streets of the past. This is the romance of Jerome as it is today. The Jerome of yesterday was tough, gritty, and peopled with hard working and hard playing miners.

Jerome Cira 1920's
Photo courtesy of The Sedona Historical Society

The Sinagua, prehistoric Indians, were the first to mine the Black Hills of Arizona a thousand years ago. Looking for blue azurite for jewelry and various ores to make pigments, they made their presence known before they left the Verde Valley in the fifteenth century. Spanish gold seekers who appeared in the late sixteenth century left empty handed. The Hills remained quiet until the late nineteenth century (1876) when Al Sieber, one of General Crook's scouts, staked a claim on the mountain. Two other prospectors, Angus McKinnon and M.A. Ruffner, filed claims at the same time. The news spread to the financiers in New York. James Douglas was sent by two Eastern financiers to check out the profitability of the ore at the site. He advised against investing. His clients went to Bisbee. Ruffner and McKinnon knew they could not finance the large scale operation needed to mine their claim. They leased it to the governor of the Arizona Territory, Frederick Tritle.

Tritle had problems. In order to get the coke from Wales to fuel the smelter to get the copper from the ore, the coke had to be shipped from Wales around Cape Horn to San Francisco. It then came by rail to Ashfork where it was unloaded into wagons for the 60 mile trip to the mine. For this he needed money. Two New York money men, James MacDonald and Eugene Jerome became partners with Tritle in the United Verde Company. Jerome (who was the uncle of Jenny Jerome, the mother of Winston Churchill) would invest only if the mining camp was named after him. (Just a bit arrogant.)

Jerome would "boom" and "bust" with the price of copper. But then the price of copper steadily climbed. Jerome exploded with population. Housing was thrown up helter skelter. In the 1890s, Jerome burned out three times in three years. In 1899, Jerome incorporated, the 5th largest city in Arizona. (Traffic up Mingus Mountain in 1919 rivals SR 179 in 2009) By 1929, the population of Jerome reached 15,000. Arizona was producing more copper than any other state…United Verde produced $29 million in ore in a single year. But then the big "bust" came. The stock market crashed, mines closed, population dwindled. Phelps Dodge, in 1935, picked up the pieces and reopened the mine. It paid off. Copper was king during World War II for shells, ships, communication equipment, etc. It wasn't until January 1953 that Jerome mining finally ceased. But Jerome was just resting — until its rebirth as a quaint, funky tourist attraction. What fun!

RANCHER, JOURNALIST, LEGISLATOR, BIG PARK PIONEER

Meet Kel Fox, an extraordinary man. Though born on the East Coast, he became the quintessential Arizona citizen. Kelvin Fox was nine when his family came to Arizona in 1922. They bought ranch land in Cornville and summer grazing land up around Munds Park near the crest of Schnebly Hill Road. The summer grazing land would eventually become "Foxboro," a camp/school without

Kel Fox
Photo courtesy of Sedona Historical Society

books "for the pampered sons of wealthy Easterners." Kel was always drawn to ranching even though he flirted with a few other careers along the way. In the 1930s, he did some wrangling and stunt work for movie companies filming in Red Rock country. According to Kel, "...stunt riders were paid from $5 to $50. You got the $50 if you were willing to take a fall."

He entered Princeton in 1931, at the beginning of the Depression. Family money was tight, and Kel helped pay his way through school. He was a stringer for several newspapers on the East Coast, as well as United Press International. During this time, he interviewed Albert Einstein and introduced the physicist to ice cream cones. He also began a weekly paper at Princeton—still published-- which allowed him to graduate with a B.A. cum laude and $2000 in his pocket. He had a full time job offer from United Press, but Kel was a rancher. He later received a doctorate in agriculture from the University of Arizona.

At age 22, Kel was living in a 10-x12 foot cabin in Big Park. For the next several years he "toughed" it out while trying to re-stock the ranch. Eventually the hard work paid off and the ranch began to prosper. He began to dabble in politics, managing Bob Jones' campaign in 1938 and serving as executive secretary to Gov. Jones. During World War II Kel was a member of the Coast Guard serving as liaison officer between the State Dept. and the Office of War Information. (Loss of a kidney in childhood kept him out of combat.) There he met Hamilton Warren and encouraged him to come to Big Park after the war. Eventually Warren built Verde Valley School.

At the war's end Kel Fox entered Arizona politics with gusto. He was a state representative from 1947 to 1953 and a senator from Yavapai County the following 2 years. He served on various commissions and boards for 50 years, including Water Quality Control, Water Resources Committee, Verde-Oak Creek Soil Conservation, and the State Board of Appeals. He and his wife Patty had 2 sons and 4 grandchildren. Kel Fox died in 1998 at age 85. Quite a man!

THE LADY JUNK COLLECTOR

Laura Purtymun McBride was many things. Known as the First Lady of the Sedona Historical Society, she was a delightful storyteller, a successful author, an oral historian, and a founder of the Sedona Historical Society. The fourth of the nine children of Clara Thompson Purtymun, she was the granddaughter of J. J. Thompson, the original Anglo settler of Oak Creek Canyon. On her father's (Purtymun) side, she was the great granddaughter of Bear Howard. In Sedona genealogy, her "pedigree" was impeccable.

She was born in Oak Creek Canyon in 1910. Laura attended both the one room school in Oak Creek Canyon and later the Red Rock School located in the hamlet of Red Rock near Oak Creek Crossing, just across the creek from Big Park. In 1924 she embarked on a remarkable journey with members of her family, beautifully recorded in her book *Traveling by Tin Lizzie*. Just before her 22nd birthday she married Ray McBride and began the unique "rest of her life."

Laura as a flapper
Photo courtesy of Sedona Historical Society

Laura was fascinated by old things: old stories, old people, old gadgets and devices. This was an interest that would continue for her entire life. When Ray lost his job with the closing of the copper smelter in the late 1930s, they moved up into Oak Creek Canyon and finally moved to the Thompson property just north of where the sand sculpture statues were (taken down about 1997). Ray built a home there from scrap lumber and tin. The inside of the house was lined with broken down cardboard boxes, and "wallpapered" with newspaper. Eventually they covered the outside of the house with tar paper to provide insulation.

That's when Laura's creativity blossomed. She began building exterior rock walls. She incorporated some unique stones, adding rocks, shells and even broken bottles. She called herself a junk collector. He would go to garbage heaps to find old bottles and containers. (A small part of her collection can still be seen at the Sedona Heritage Museum.) Broken articles that had sentimental value were given to Laura, rather than thrown away. Half of a pink poodle, it's in Laura's wall. A piece of china showing the Last Supper, Vietnamese dishes broken in a barroom fight, they were all in Laura's walls. After hundreds of yards of walls filled with interesting "stuff" were built, she began to create walking paths, and rock art...all made from pieces of broken pottery and glass given to her by family and friends. Rock walls about four feet high wound throughout the property. The homestead even included a Laura-made gold fish pond with a small waterfall, and a little house encased in rock. Some of her creativity must have rubbed off on Ray. He built wind toys and wind chimes from bottles and tin cans and decorated the trees around the house.

Laura was active, energetic and creative until she died in July of 1994. She enjoyed being a junk collector even more than being the First Lady of Sedona.

LENA DICKIE, HORSEWOMAN EXTRAORDINAIRE!

Lena Dickie 1987
Photo courtesy of Sedona Historical Society

Sedona has had more than its share of interesting women. If you heard the name Schnebly, Schuerman, Thompson or Gulick, you had a pretty good idea of who she was and how she fit into Sedona's past. A delightful, colorful character from Sedona's more recent past probably had a lot more fun than did the aforementioned ladies. And, unfortunately, you may never have heard of her. So allow me to enlighten you.

Lena Dickie was born in Michigan and spent many of her early years there. Her father was a horse trainer, and she took to it naturally. By the time she left her teen years she traveled with a rodeo as a trick rider with her trick horse

Tarzan. She was known as Rodeo Rose and her horse Tarzan. At one time she had trained her trick horse, Lad, to jump through a fire hoop! But horses were not quite enough for Lena. She began to train Chihuahuas to pull a miniature stagecoach. (She was no bigger than a minute herself.) All the equipment she used was hand made by Lena. She took her troupe to 45 states as well as Mexico and Canada.

After she was widowed in 1961 (her late husband was a veterinarian), Lena moved to Phoenix where she managed a commercial kennel that could accommodate 99 dogs. She discovered Sedona and fell in love with it. In 1970 she moved here and began training horses for Bob Eggert. This time they were miniature horses as well as quarter horses. She was featured in national equine magazines for her skill and talent.

Lena always had a flair for the dramatic. She was really a show "man" at heart. She lived and worked in Big Park where, during the 1970s, she would startle some of the locals by riding her red sulky pulled by her horse Tahzay down to pick up the mail.

In the course of her career Lena earned many honors. She was crowned "Queen of the Rodeo" twice, once in Muskegon in the 1930s and once in Sedona in 1993. She is in the Cowgirl Hall of Fame, and was a regular in every St. Patrick's Day Parade except the first one. Lena, along with her dog Sundancer, was the Grand Marshal of the 1997 parade. She garnered almost 90 trophies from the various events. All you had to do to get Lena in a parade was ask her. She loved the parades, and her animals (from miniature Chihuahuas to Great Danes, from miniature horses to full sized American Saddle Breds) apparently loved them, too. They always performed brilliantly.

Lena was the forerunner of the "energizer bunny." In her late eighties and early nineties she had no qualms about taking off alone and driving to Colorado or Wyoming to show off her miniature friends. Lena was in her mid-nineties when she got her driver's license renewed! I had the privilege of meeting and talking with her shortly after I moved to Sedona, and I must tell you I was impressed. Lena died in 2006 at the age of 101. What a gal!!

RESORT TIME

The Sedona area has four recognized periods of settlement and growth. The first was the time of the Oak Creek Canyon homesteaders — the farmers: Thompsons, Purtymuns, and Schnebleys. Then came the orchard growers: the Jordans and the Pendleys. The third major period included the ranchers and — to some extent — sheepherders. Finally, there came the artistic set: movie makers, artists, sculptors, crafters. There was something that held these groups together. Hospitality! From Schnebleys first "bed and breakfast" near the present Los Abrigados to today's Hilton Resort in the Village, travelers were made welcome. Tourism became the fifth and greatest industry in Sedona.

During the '20s and '30s, optimistic families built cabins and lodges to offer shelter to the hundreds of tourists making their way to Sedona. Each has his own story. Some were successful, many were not.

Ray Simpson moved west from Kansas to Flagstaff to open the J.C. Penney Store. At the same time he purchased a parcel of 80 acres in Oak Creek Canyon consisting of a small lodge and an apple orchard (now the parking lot for West Fork hikers). Ray was pretty sharp. He purchased the property for taxes owed, and he re-named the lodge the Call of the Canyon to take advantage of the publicity generated by the movie filmed there in 1923. The property was expanded to include a general store, gas station and seven summer rental cabins. But the big draw was the Olympic sized swimming pool, the only public swimming pool in northern Arizona during the 1930s and '40s.

In the mid 1930s, Ray's son Willard went to school at Texas Tech University in Lubbock. He met and eventually brought home a pretty Texas Tech co-ed Lillian (Miss Dairy

Queen of 1935). She was quite an attraction. They married in 1937, and the beauty queen showed that she knew how to work. One of the major chores was cleaning the huge swimming pool every Sunday. It was drained, scrubbed and filled in with water from Oak Creek, ready for another week of tourists.

Lillian Simpson(Miss Dairy Queen 1935)
Photo Courtesyof Bud and Gail Simpson

The Call of the Canyon was sold during World War II. The young Simpsons left the area and Willard went into the Navy. After the war, they returned to Flagstaff, but they had the hospitality business in their blood. They moved to Sedona in 1951, bought 8 acres along Hwy. 89A — where Safeway is located today — for $5,000. The Simpsons built an 8-unit adobe motel that they named End O'Day Motel. It was a losing struggle to make the property profitable. Before they lost it, they were able to sell the property, and move to the Navajo Reservation where they opened a Texaco station and grocery store. In 1973 they retired to Oak Creek Canyon. After Willard's death, Lillian moved to the Village of Oak Creek. Eventually, the Call of the Canyon Resort was turned into a government parking lot. In 1982 the End O'Day Motel was torn down. Lillian celebrated her 94th birthday in August, 2009, still as delightful as when she was Miss Dairy Queen. Time marches on!

LIVING HISTORY-COWBOY CHARLEY

Charlie Piper
Photo courtesy of Judy Krueger

We all enjoy catching a glimpse of the past—how it was here not so long ago. Red Rock Country has been fortunate to have its early citizens record the way it was. Laura McBride described life here in the 1920s. Ruth Jordan and Bud Purtymun wrote their recollections of growing up in Red Rock Country. The Sedona Westerners put together a bible of life in greater Sedona in the beginning years. These are priceless, but how do we make history live for the children? It is a "prime directive" of the Sedona Historical Society to let these young citizens feel what it was like here, not so long ago. The Sedona Heritage Museum educates fourth graders throughout the Verde Valley from Flagstaff to Phoenix. Dedicated volunteers--old-timers and newcomers--staff "Pioneer Days," the living history presented to middle school children.

One such volunteer was Charley Piper, sometimes known as Cowboy Charley. Charley never earned his living as a cowboy, but his was a cowboy spirit. You look at him with his handle bar moustache and slightly bowed legs, and you would swear he lived his life on horseback. Charley is a second generation Red Rock citizen. He was born in Clemenceau (now part of Cottonwood) in 1936. He grew up in Little Horse Park, now known as the Chapel area. His parents were dry farm homesteaders. Charley and his four brothers climbed the red rocks, skated at the rink in Indian Gardens, swam in Oak Creek, and watched westerns being filmed in the area, some on their land. They enjoyed the school dances, and also enjoyed "borrowing" chickens and watermelons from neighbors. He loved the homestead — he and his brothers chiseled the family brand RX on the rocks-- and never did forgive Marguerite Staude for building the Chapel of the Holy Cross on his playground. He spent four years in the Air Force, came back to Arizona, married and had five children. He made a good living as a welder and mechanic, but it was later he discovered his creative side. Charley's gift was working with metal. He could make things with horseshoes, could take an old saw blade or a piece of scrap metal and turn it into bowie knives or spurs that are works of art.

Charley found joy in passing on the spirit of the cowboy to the youngsters who come to the Heritage Museum for Pioneer Days. He got to play cowboy and show, first hand, to hundreds of students the purposes of the cowboy tools: the hat, chaps, boots, spurs and the gun. The museum staff would call the police department to warn them that the shots coming from Uptown were blanks and were a demonstration. The kids learned about branding, and each one got to take a brand home. Each child learned a live history lesson that would not be forgotten. Cowboy Charley died on January 19, 2009 to become part of the history he loved.

THE LOYS OF LOY CANYON

Like Rodney Dangerfield, the very early settlers of Sedona's Red Rock Country—Samuel Loy and his progeny—seem to get no respect. The Loy family was most responsible for the building of Schnebly Hill Road, but you see whose name the road carries. How did this faux pas happen?

Samuel Loy, the family patriarch, was born in 1820. Records seem to be unclear in the family log as to whether that was in Virginia or Ohio! In 1849 he headed west to California as a farmer, not a prospector. Nonetheless, he returned home four years later loaded with gold. (Those miners had to eat.) He married Jane Sinnette and moved to Missouri where he continued farming while he and Jane raised five children: James, John, William and Mary (twins), and Harriet.

Myron "Budge" Loy with his wife

In 1876, Samuel got a little restless, sold his farm, gathered up his family and joined a wagon train heading out to Oregon. But he had heard so many stories about the fertile Verde Valley that he changed his mind and headed here instead. Samuel was one of the first to settle here, before the Schuermans, the Purtymuns, and certainly before the Schneblys. He hauled freight from Phoenix to Prescott to Camp Verde on trails that would make the present Schnebly Hill Road look like I-17. The Loy family had large real estate holdings, hence we have Loy Canyon, Loy Trail, and Loy Butte.

Schnebly Hill Road came about through the persistence of John Loy. He began construction of the road in 1896. It originally was a cattle trail begun by Jim Mund (John's brother-in-law). Through John's efforts and those of the early pioneers, using picks and shovels, they got a semblance of a road going. It was first called the Verde Cut-Off Road. In 1902 the Coconino Board of Supervisors awarded a $600 contract to Jim Thompson to improve the road. The hardy souls he hired worked 12-hour days at $1.00 per day for six months to do just that. It was called "Mund's Road" and it cut the time to get from Sedona to Flagstaff in half—from 4 days to 2 days!

Although Carl Schnebly had little to do with building the road it eventually took on his name. Travelers from Flagstaff coming down the mountain to the Verde Valley found themselves near the Schnebly home (Sedona's first bed and breakfast/hotel). Soon the road became associated with the Schnebly name, and evolved into Schnebly Hill Road.

A little humor. The Loy progeny were Westerners. Myron "Budge" Loy, grandson of Samuel, would recall his WWI experience with chagrin. The Army, in its infinite wisdom, sent this Arizona cowboy to Fort Dix, New Jersey where he was transferred to the armored division and was expected to "herd" a truck down a street in New York City. Enough! He transferred to remount where he was breaking mules. At last something he knew about. The men floated down a river near Hoboken where there were about 700 horses on each barge, each horse with a serial number on its hoof. His job was to get down and authenticate each number. Fortunately the war ended, and Budge came back home to Arizona where he belonged..

MARCUS J. LAWRENCE – The Man

If you have lived in the Sedona area for more than two or three years, you remember when the Verde Valley Medical Center was known as the Marcus J. Lawrence Medical Center. I sometimes wondered who this man was who had a hospital named for him. Was he a famous doctor or researcher, or was he a philanthropist, a do-gooder? When I started to research Marcus J. Lawrence, the man, I found out that his story read like a "made for T.V. movie." It is a fascinating tale of booze, adultery, mayhem, and ultimately, homicide. Surprisingly, the facts of his life are not too readily available. But this is what I was able to glean from old accounts in the Prescott Daily Courier; "Inside Detective;" "True Detective Mysteries;" The Sedona Historical Society, the Internet, and especially the "history wall" at the Verde Valley Medical Center.

Marcus J. Lawrence was a handsome man, the son of a wealthy Cleveland, Ohio family, who moved to the Verde Valley with his mother, Carrie Lawrence, in 1931. They had lived in Washington, D.C. for a short while, but not much is recorded of his life there. He was described as shy and quiet by those who knew him, but also described as a philandering playboy by lurid detective and true crime magazines of the day. In December, 1933, Lawrence and his partner Bruce Brockett bought the V Bar V Cattle Company located near Big Park and Camp Verde. He reportedly stated it was the kind of business where he wouldn't have to meet too many people. Sometime between 1930 and 1936 he married, but his wife is not really a part of his story. Lawrence kept going back and forth to D.C. although he and his wife were estranged. They had no children. By 1937 divorce proceedings were in place. And Lawrence did not feel the need to live as a monk. He was a young adult during the Roaring Twenties and he knew how to party. He did find other available means of fulfillment.

Lawrence got involved with some of the wilder element in Prescott and with the easy going night life along Whiskey Row. He developed a friendship with Ernesto Lira and his mistress, the still married Odessa Webb. Lira owned several bars and gambling houses on the Row. In a three month period they became very friendly. So friendly that Lawrence would often stay at Lira and Odessa's home in Prescott.

Lawrence often went back East, but renewed the friendship easily when he returned to Arizona. Odessa, who was a very pretty woman, had been a waitress when she met Lira, but left her husband and went off to live with the wealthy bar owner. They lived together as husband and wife. Lira said he planned to marry her whenever it was possible. Most of their friends believed that, indeed, they would marry whenever Odessa was divorced sometime in the future. Lawrence and Odessa met in March of 1938 when they were introduced by Lira. The three formed a little clique that hosted many private parties that included the doers and shakers of Arizona in the Thirties.

Odessa's 27th birthday was on May 10, 1938. A celebration was held in Lira's home. There were a number of people present with a good bit of drinking going on for several hours. However, when Lawrence said he was tired and went to bed at the house, people began to leave. Soon after, Odessa and a girlfriend went into town and Lira headed to the Tivoli Club, one of the bars he owned.

Lira had become suspicious over the previous few weeks about just how friendly Lawrence and Odessa actually were. He believed they were having an affair. Why not catch them in the act? He went into his office, grabbed a camera, and told his manager to tell anyone who asked that he (Lira) was working in his office and did not want to be disturbed. Lira then went home, quietly slipped into the house, and hid in a bedroom closet—not the bedroom occupied by Lawrence.

He heard Odessa come into the house alone. He also heard her call the Tivoli and ask for him. When she was told that he could not be disturbed, she believed all was safe. She went into Lawrence's bedroom. Lira then burst into the room, waving his camera and a shotgun. No one is sure exactly happened—even to this day—but there is agreement that Lira beat the pair with his camera and with the barrel of the shotgun. Lawrence was badly beaten. Little is known about the extent of Odessa's injuries. We do know that the camera was shattered and the walls were bloodied.

When Lira finally realized the extent of Lawrence's injuries, he called for a doctor. According to testimony, Dr. Ernest Born made three visits to the Lira home that night before he called for an ambulance to take Lawrence to the hospital. Lawrence died en route of a massive brain hemorrhage.

Lira was arrested and went to trial in the summer of 1938. The prosecution alleged that Lira was planning extortion and blackmail of Lawrence (taking the camera was proof of that) and the killing happened during the perpetration of a felony. The defense countered that it was an accident and the victim died because the doctor didn't address his injuries in a timely manner. During the course of the trial, Odessa did admit that she and Marcus had been involved in a physical affair and had liaisons in several places in the Prescott/Cottonwood area, including one at the Little Pig Restaurant in Cottonwood, which sat on the present location of the Verde Valley Medical Center. The jury believed the prosecution and on July 16, 1938, Lira was found guilty of second degree murder and sentenced from twenty to forty years in prison. Fortunately for Mr. Lira, in 1943, Governor Sidney Preston Osborn commuted his sentence, and he was a free man after having served five years.

Carrie Lawrence, the mother of Marcus, wished to memorialize her son in some way. She thought about naming a bridge after him, but Dr. A. C. Carlson convinced her that a more fitting memorial would be the creation of a medical clinic. On June 2, 1939, what was to become the Marcus J. Lawrence Medical Center –and eventually the Verde Valley Medical Center--began as a small outpatient clinic. Today it is one of the largest employers in the Verde Valley with a 99 bed capacity and a staff of more than 600. All of it a memorial to a murdered son.

MAYHEW'S – WHAT IS IT?

Have you hiked the West Fork Trail in Oak Creek Canyon? Were you intrigued by the skeletal remains of a building at the junction of the West Fork and Oak Creek? What you see is all that is left of the resort known as Mayhew's Oak Creek Lodge, listed in the National Register of Historic Places. Its guest register included Clark Gable, James Stewart, Herbert Hoover and other notables, as well as foreign dignitaries, such as the British ambassador from Great Britain. It had grown from a homesteader's cabin to hideaway for the rich and famous. How did that come about?

Mayhew's Lodge
Photo courtesy of Sedona Historical Society

Bear Howard, one of our colorful pioneers, built a one room cabin in that spot in 1880. Oak Creek Canyon was a good place to hide from the lawmen who were after him. A few years later he sold the property to a man by the name of Thomas. Thomas' son Lew took over the property, and in 1895 built a two story log house about twelve feet away from the original cabin. He and his wife Rosa started taking in summer boarders. Lew Thomas died about 1920 and the property passed to his heirs. About four years later, James Lamport of Flagstaff bought the property from the heirs . His son George reopened the lodge and kept boarders. It was now called "The Tioga." Two years later the property was sold to Carl Mayhew who enlarged the building, made a number of improvements, and renamed it Mayhew's Oak Creek Lodge.

Carl Mayhew was a professional photographer who saw combat during World War I. He was badly gassed, losing one lung, and ended up in the milder climate of Flagstaff. In 1925, he accompanied film maker Jesse Lasky down Oak Canyon to prepare to film the Zane Grey movie "Call of the Canyon." Part of it was to be done at Bear Howard's old cabin, now a lodge. Mayhew fell in love with the place and bought the 40 acre property at West Fork.

The lodge was very primitive. There were no electric lights, no inside plumbing, and even the bath was outdoors. Fruits and vegetables were kept in a spring house that had cool water running through it. There was only a rough trail, and the round trip to Sedona took a day and a half. It took two days to make the round trip to Flagstaff. Carl kept adding to and improving the lodge; his wife's culinary skills became famous. Carl died in 1943, but the lodge continued to thrive under the management of his wife, daughter and son-in-law. By the forties and fifties the resort had an international reputation. The road through the canyon was paved in the late 1930s. The lodge could be reached all summer long.

By 1968 the family was ready to retire. They sold the property to the Forest Service. The Service decided it would cost $500,000 to restore the lodge as a museum. So they boarded it up. In March, 1980, Mayhew's Oak Creek Lodge burned to the ground. A terrible loss to historic preservation.

THE MURDERING MADAM

Whiskey Row in Prescott has a reputation for producing colorful characters, but one of those characters was especially outrageous. Gabriell Dollie Wiley (known as Gabe) had the good fortune to marry men who conveniently died and left her financially well off, or at least free to marry again. In her mind, she just did what a gal had to do.

Gabriell Dardley was born in 1890 or 1891 and by 1906 she was working as a prostitute in the mining camps of Nevada. She claimed she was born in Italy (or maybe France) and found her way, one way or another, to San Francisco where she lived until the 1906 earthquake and fire. While that city was reeling from the disaster, she moved on.

Gabe met up with a group heading east to Nevada. She worked in eateries during day and turned tricks at night. She obviously did well financially. By the age of 18 she was living on Whiskey Row in Prescott where she was a very popular and successful hooker. Just a few years later, in 1915, she became a household name. Her abusive pimp (these weren't words that had ever appeared in newspapers back then) Leonard Topp proposed to her. That night, after she agreed to marry him, he sent her back out on the streets while he stole her diamond jewelry and took off for California with another woman. Well, Gabe had enough. She hunted him down. Gabe spotted him in a liquor store. She walked in, hands inside a fur muff, and said "Hello, Leonard." He turned around, and she shot him with the gun she held inside the muff.

She became a darling of the press. Her defense attorney was Earl Rogers, the outstanding criminal attorney of his time. Rogers' daughter, Adela Rogers St. John (some of you readers may remember her name) took it upon herself to make Gabe a heroine. And the public ate it up. The district attorney may have had a rock solid case against her, but he didn't stand a chance. In eight minutes time, the all male jury found her Not Guilty.

Gabriell Dardley
Photo courtesy of the Sedona Historical Society

By 1920 Gabe was back in Prescott, this time running the show. She was a savvy entrepreneur, owning the business, the girls, and even a hotel — the Rex Arms Hotel. According to various sources, there were at least six men who died under questionable circumstances as a result of their dalliances with Gabe.

Actually, as a result of one of her crusades, lawmakers wrote one of this country's first privacy laws. Gabe had ambled over to watch a silent movie "The Red Kimona." Lo and behold, it was her life on screen, using her real name! Without telling her!! Even though the film was sympathetic to her, Gabe sued the filmmakers for invasion of privacy and won. She was awarded $50,000, big money in those days.

Gabe continued her very successful business in Prescott. In 1937, nearing the age of fifty, she married George Wiley, an ex-bootlegger. They moved to Salome (near Quartzite). He didn't seem to mind that she continued in the "Madam" business, as long as he wasn't involved. But in November of 1940 George and Gabe had a bang up argument, supposedly related to her business. When George did not show up for lunch at their restaurant, a hired hand found his body at their home. Near his body was a partly full glass of water mixed with cynogas, a form of cyanide. The official ruling was suicide.

Gabe never married again (thank heaven). She died on Christmas Day 1962, and is buried in Prescott.

NAVAJO ORDNANCE DEPOT- BOOM TOWN

Flagstaff, Arizona, was one of the few towns that managed to hold its own during the Great Depression. Monies from the CCC Camps, WPA, and National Highway Recovery Program kept the town gainfully employed. Not so for the town of Bellemont, Flagstaff's tiny neighbor ten miles to the west. In the summer of 1941 its population had dropped to fewer than 60 people, including five ladies of the evening who worked in one of the few successful enterprises in the town.

Quietly, in August of 1941, a small group of strangers from the War Department came to inspect the area around Bellemont. Europe was in full scale war. There were rumblings of problems in the Pacific. The men were scouting for an appropriate site to construct an ammunition depot. The land around Flagstaff, and especially Bellemont, fit the criteria. Come December 7, 1941, the rush was on.

The $17 million project ($175 million in today's dollars) would cover 48 square miles and require a labor pool of 6000 construction workers, with a permanent work force of 2000. The population of Flagstaff jumped from 5000 to 20,000 almost overnight. Named the Flagstaff Ordnance Depot, the facility would be the key back up storage depot for the Port of Los Angeles. But where would they find the workers to build the project? The armed services were taking most of the available men.

The army went to the nearby Navajo reservation to recruit workers. In February of 1942 the War Department renamed the facility the Navajo Ordnance Depot to honor (and flatter?) those who would build and work in the depot. The commander worked with the Native American leaders, and after some false starts, invited the Navajo and Hopi workers to build an "Indian Village" right on the base. Would you believe…for the first time in history, about 3500 Native Americans chose to live on a military base behind wire fences. They built hogans and modern family units, trading posts, schools for the children and recreational facilities. The work force was not limited to men. Indian women took advantage of the good wages and worked right along with the men. About a third of the work force was female. The women worked with ammunition, repairing 500 pound bombs, rewiring 1000 pound bombs. Others worked on grenades. They drove semi-trucks and school buses. Wow! They could do it all.

As World War II was coming to an end in early 1945, 250 Austrian POWs were moved from the prisoner of war camp in Florence, AZ to the Navajo Depot. They worked in all areas of the camp, except those directly involving munitions. The Austrians were fascinated with the Indian culture, and worked well with the Native American workers. A unique situation — no where else in the country did prisoners of war work peacefully with Native Americans.

This fascinating history was gleaned from ARIZONA'S WAR TOWN, Flagstaff, Navajo Ordnance Depot, and World War II, by John S. Westerlund. It's a great read.

THE PIONEER STONE MASON

As you make your way through the Red Rock area, your eye is caught by the early houses built by the pioneers. These are neither the tent houses nor the wood cabins, but the houses built from the red rocks that encompass the area. How did these come about? Who had the talent to create these homes before architects discovered Red Rock Country?

The original pioneer stone mason was a fascinating character. No one was exactly sure where he came from — although folks knew he was of German descent. And no one knew what happened to him — he just kind of disappeared sometime around 1920. His name was Nick Kinney.

Sherman Loy, a grandson of Henry Schuerman, tells of the stories his grandfather told about Nick. You see, Nick was a bit of a sot. He did like his alcohol. But he had an unbelievable talent working with stone. Not only did he build the houses, but he actually quarried the rock. Many of the houses are still standing today.

Henry Schuerman was the original settler (in 1885) of the hamlet of Red Rock, across the creek from Big Park, which had a name and a small population several years before Camp Garden became Sedona. When Henry wanted Nick to do some work for him, he would head up to Jerome (Nick's stomping ground) find him, toss him in a wagon and bring him down to Red Rock, clean him up and sober him up, (See photo of a cleaned up Nick) and set him to the task of home construction. Nick could cut and square up those rocks, mortar them up with lime and sand (cement was not available), and build a house that would last for as long as a century.

Nick Kinney
Photo and history courtesy of Sherman Loy, Jake Weber and the Sedona Historical Society

Nick built his first house for Henry Schuerman about 1902, which unfortunately was later taken in an Oak Creek flood. He also did the stone work on the Ambrosio Chavez homestead, the blacksmith shop at Crescent Moon Park, the fireplace and chimney at the Schuerman homestead house, the Tom Chavez homestead house, all of which are still standing. The two houses he built on the Erwin Schuerman homestead and the George Jordan house in what is now Uptown Sedona are gone.

However, Old Nick would be pleased to know that the stone house he built on the Ambrosio Armijo homestead is in beautiful shape. It was lovingly restored by Jake Weber and is on the State and National Registers of Historic Places. Good work, Nick!

OWENBY – A FIRST FAMILY OF SEDONA

Frank Owenby
Photo courtesy Sedona Historical Society

The Frank Owenby family emigrated from Texas to Colorado to Arizona about 1885. They arrived in Flagstaff in 1889, the year the Babbitt brothers opened their first store. Frank was an entrepreneur at heart. He saw a need and filled it. Flagstaff was growing, and since there was no water system of any kind, unless the residents had their own wells, they had no water. Frank began his water business, delivering water by wagon from the town spring to the individual homes. While he was in the water business, he got a few head of cows and started a small dairy. He could deliver milk as well as water on his route. The dairy cows kept increasing, and soon he had a fair sized herd of cattle.

Now Frank was a cattle man at heart...had been one in Texas. He wanted to be one again in Arizona. After scouting the country around Flagstaff — in all directions — the Oak Creek area around present day Sedona looked good to him. In 1893 the Owenby family (Frank and Nancy, 3 sons and 1 daughter) headed down the Old Verde Road (approximately the route of I-17, but unpaved) to the Beaver Head station (just south of the Village of Oak Creek), then north through Big Park into the environs of present day Sedona. He filed a homestead on some land across the creek from the present King's Ransom Motel. The homestead had originally been filed on by Bill James, son of Abraham James, the first Sedona homesteader. Filing and trading and selling homestead claims was a fact of life among the early pioneers. Frank Owenby was no exception. He proved up on this first homestead and actually got a patent on the property, the first in Sedona. Over the course of years he sold and bought several homesteads, ending in 1908 with what became the George Jordan place in Sedona (present day Art Barn).

Frank Owenby began the irrigation ditch system which still bears his name. It serves almost 2 dozen properties between Los Abrigados and L'Auberge.

Schooling was important to these early settlers, and they made adjustments in their lifestyle in order to accommodate that priority. The closest school was on the Schuerman ranch in Red Rock (across the creek from Big Park), so part of the year was spent there. Other times they moved to Cornville for the school term. It was amazing how well educated these youngsters became with this "catch as catch can" kind of learning.

In 1901, after obtaining the patent on his first 80 acre homestead, Owenby sold the property to D.E. Schnebly, the brother of T.C. and Sedona Schnebly. Son Roy Owenby married one of the Schuerman daughters in 1910. In 1915, Frank Owenby sold his Sedona cattle to Lee Van Deren, and his Sedona ranch to Jess Purtymun. He moved to Adamana (now a ghost town in western Apache County) to get back into the cattle business with his son Ira. He lived there until his death in 1937.

ARIZONA – ROMANCE OF THE WEST?

Through the "brainwashing" of western movies, most of us were caught up in the romance of the Old West. The movies never exposed the audience to the dirt, hard work and monotony of existence at the frontier. If you needed a doctor, well, good luck. There were very few medical men back then, and no medical women except for midwives and a few nurses. Here in Red Rock country, there were two hospitals available – sort of. One was in Flagstaff and the other in Jerome. But according to Albert Thompson, the one in Jerome was far superior to the one in Flagstaff. If you were smart you opted for the Jerome Hospital which was funded and run by the United Verde Mining Company. Definitely upscale!

Of course, back then going to any hospital was definitely a last resort. Even calling a doctor was only done in cases of broken bones, blood poisoning or snake bite. Otherwise mom was the attending physician. Did you get a cut on an arm or leg? Just dab on a little turpentine. And for a sore throat you just rubbed the turpentine on your neck. A cure for chest congestion might even work today, if you could live through the treatment. Melt lard with kerosene and turpentine to a temperature as hot as you can stand. Pour it on a flannel cloth and place that on your chest and another one on your back. Women took up smoking not for the pleasure of nicotine, but tobacco smoke alleviated toothache pain! Supposedly, tobacco smoke blown into a child's ear would sooth an earache.

It's always fun to look at some of the stories of an area's past and try to figure out what is truth and what is a tall story. One tale that was popular for quite a while is that Zane Grey, the Louis L'Amour of his day, had a cabin at West Fork on Oak Creek. Not so. (For those of you who are too young to remember, Zane Grey is known as the father of the western novel.) According to William Howard, Grey did spend some time in the Lolomai Lodge, which is on the banks of Oak Creek, but he never built a cabin there. The only cabin built near West Fork at that time was constructed by the folks filming an "oater" in the Canyon. They used it for the movie, but tore it down when they were through with it. So Zane Grey was only a temporary visitor to the area — where he wrote some fine stories — but was never a permanent resident.

Again, trivia time. The town of Snowflake did not get its name because of fluffy white precipitation falling on it. It was named after the two founding Mormon bishops, Erastus Snow and William Flake.

For those of you adventurous enough to visit the United Verde Hospital in Jerome, it is now a fine hotel and dining establishment. The Jerome Grand Hotel is noted not just for its fine cuisine, but also for suspected paranormal activity. Woo-woo.

FRONTIER WIVES

I know that I would not have lasted more than six weeks living on the frontier. I also know that it was women who were the civilizing elements in the westward settlement. I really am in awe of the women who stayed here...the homestead wives who made homes and raised families here in the Arizona Territory. Two women need to be recognized as unsung heroines in the settlement of Red Rock Country, Elizabeth Ragsdale James and Margaret (sometimes called Margrett) James Thompson. So here's a "huzzah" for these special women.

Elizabeth Ragsdale, born in 1828, married Abraham James, born in 1823, a "hard luck" wanderer who moved his brood from one place to another throughout the west, from Arkansas to Texas, Missouri, California, eventually finding his way to Arizona. Elizabeth's oldest child, Louisa, was born in 1847, her youngest, David, was born in 1868. And there were six in between, including Maggie. Elizabeth spent much of her life making a home for her family under trying circumstances. It's what you did if you were a woman married to a wanderer. She was also the stereotype of a frontier woman—she was an inveterate pipe smoker! A friend of Abraham's, Jim Thompson—another hard luck wanderer, had invited him to make his way to the Verde Valley. In 1878 the Jameses became the first homesteaders in what would become Sedona. Abraham is credited with naming Courthouse Rock, Bell Rock, Steamboat Rock and Table Mountain. Along the way, Elizabeth acquired a number of skills that stood her in good stead, especially midwifery. The midwife would come and stay for a week or two before the expected birth. Among the children she helped deliver were those born to Doretta Schuerman. It's a good thing she had this talent because in 1881 Abraham died, and Elizabeth and her children were left to run the homestead…and make do as they could. In 1891 Elizabeth married old Bear Howard, a marriage that lasted 3 months. She didn't like sleeping with his dogs and she didn't like him giving away her cattle. She went back to the farm with one of her sons and lived until 1905.

Margaret (Maggie) Paralee James was born in 1864. She was the sixth of nine children. Abraham and Jim Thompson had become friends while they were both in Nevada. Maggie was 14 years old when the James family moved to the Camp Garden area (present day Sedona). Jim and the James family were close. There weren't many people in the area. Jim was past due to settle down and Maggie was approaching marriage age. Was it romance or was it convenience? The barely 16 year old Maggie married 38 year old Jim in 1880. Maggie had worked hard her whole young life. She had barely six months of formal schooling, but she taught herself to read and write. She was prepared for the tough life here on the frontier. Like her mother, Maggie had nine children, the oldest born in 1882 and the youngest born in 1911. Think about it. Maggie was pregnant off and on for 30 years. Jim had not overcome his wanderlust, and he was gone a lot, but he always came back. Maggie stayed on the land. She tended the kids, the gardens, the cattle and the pigs. She cooked, preserved food, and raised all nine children to adulthood. Jim died in 1917 when the youngest child was six years old. (That's when Maggie started sneaking cigarettes.) She died in 1936, honored and respected by her family and her friends.

POLLUTION...IN THE OLD DAYS

For those of you who believe air pollution is a late 20th century problem, read on. Prosperity for a few can often bring problems for the many. This was the case in the early part of the 20th century right here in Red Rock Country. Copper mining in Jerome made it the 4th largest city in the state, with a population of 15,000. Money was pouring into the coffers of the eastern industrialists while the local farmers were trying to hold their own against the encroachment of the industrial age.

United Verde Copper Company Smelter
Photo courtesy of Sedona Historical Society

Will Jordan, Sr., a farmer near Clarkdale and Jerome, was bought out by the United Verde Copper Company. The company had moved its smelter from Jerome downhill, and had bought up several farms for the expansion. Will worked as a superintendent for the company, running the farm. This lasted for a year or two until he got disgusted with the operation. It was time to go out on his own again. As soon as Will left, the company broke ground for a new smelter on the Jordan farm. The first furnace went into operation in 1915.

Will took no chances when buying the new farm. He checked with a superintendent of the smelter to determine how far down valley the smoke would harm crops. He was told it would be about 3 miles. So he and his sons bought land in the Bridgeport area, 9 miles down valley. The first smoke came out of the smelter in May, 1915, and by September, they could smell the smoke and see the haze. The smoke being spewed out had a high concentration of sulfur dioxide, which, when it mixed with the dew that settled at night, produced sulfuric acid. Just 2 years later another smelter was built in Clemenceau (part of present day Cottonwood). Newspaper headlines proclaimed "Smelter smoke is ruining valley vegetation." Cattlemen were being affected, as well as farmers and orchardists. Grazing for the cattle was limited by the toxic smoke.

The farmers organized — 110 of them. On August 17, 1920, suit was filed in Yavapai County against United Verde and the United Verde Extension Mining Company. Eventually, this would be one of the first air pollution suits to be heard in the U.S. Supreme Court. Litigation went on for years. The farmers were a pretty savvy group. They devised a method to suck up some of the polluted air into a bottle and then test it for noxious elements. They collected blighted alfalfa and baled it for evidence. Their arguments proved to be stronger than the copper companies' delaying tactics.

Justice of a sort finally prevailed. The farmers won their case in 1924, but only for a third of what they should have received. The companies kept appealing the judgment, but finally gave up. The last smelter closed in 1951. However, the farmers did get some money. Will Jordan and his sons bought land in Sedona, 20 miles from the smelter. And they prospered.

(Ruth Jordan Van Epp's book: <u>Following Their Westward Star</u> for an in depth study)

MUSINGS OF A PURTYMUN WIFE

Clara (Thompson) Purtymun with
husband Albert and daughter Delia

Photo courtesy of the Sedona Historical Society

Clara Thompson was born in 1887, the third child of
J.J. and Maggie Thompson. J.J. (or Jim) was the original
homesteader in Oak Creek Canyon. Albert Purtymun, born
in 1881, was the son of Stephen and Mattie Purtymun, and
the grandson of "Bear" Howard. Both the Thompson Clan
and the Purtymun Clan were pretty prolific, so is it any
wonder that the two Thompson daughters married two of
the Purtymun sons? You married who was available. (As a

little tidbit of trivia, another Purtymun brother, Jess, ran the best still in Oak Creek Canyon—before, during and after Prohibition. He was famous for them, and Bootlegger Campground was named for him.) Life was neither easy nor comfortable in the wilds of Northern Arizona at the turn of the twentieth century (1900). Fortunately, for those of us living generations later, Clara put down in her own words a record of her life and times.

Clara was born just under the hill where the King's Ransom Hotel is now, long before the Schneblys made their way to the area. For the first few years of her life she and her family lived at the Indian Gardens homestead. J.J. had to travel away from home much of the time for various jobs so Maggie had the task of raising the children. Since there was no school in the Canyon, when it was time for their education to begin, the family moved to Red Rock to attend the school on the Henry Schuerman place. School went from March through August since winter travel was "iffy" at best. Clara was so little that the teacher arranged a place for her to take a nap every day. Starting in the first grade the pupils learned arithmetic, reading, language, spelling, geography and copybooks (a form of penmanship). Quite a load of learning for the youngsters!

Early marriage was the custom. When Clara was sixteen she married Albert Purtymun who was twenty-two. Albert was a woodcutter who moved from job to job, but he also worked as a miner when he could find the work. Much of the time they lived in a tent. At one point in their work-related traverses Albert told Clara he had a nice place for her to live in. When she got there she saw a square hole dug in the ground, a fireplace on one end, and a tent over the top! Their first child, Delia, was born in the spring of 1904. Clara had another child every two to three years until the ninth child, Zola, was born in 1925. All told, there were seven girls and two boys. All but one girl lived to adulthood.

Purtymun daughter No. 4 was Laura Purtymun (McBride) who recounted their amazing 1924 trek to California via New Mexico, Colorado, Utah, Idaho, and Oregon in her memoir TRAVELING BY TIN LIZZIE. It took them six months one way. The Purtymuns were used to making do, doing without, and making the best of it.

Clara Purtymun was almost too good to believe. She put up with the constant moving, the uncertainty of work, a passel of kids to raise, and the hardships of a pioneer life. She was tough. She had to be. She died in 1982. Much of the credit for the settlement and civilizing of the West goes to women like Clara Thompson Purtymun.

RECOLLECTIONS FROM THE OLD TIMERS

How did Schnebly Hill Road come to be? It was first a people trail between Munds Park and Jerome and then a cattle trail, one that was used by Big Park ranchers to get their herds up to the top of the Mogollon Rim. The cattle summered there. Since the trail led to Munds Park, it became known as the Munds Trail. As early as 1896, this became the obvious way to shortcut the six day wagon trip from Red Rock/Big Park to Flagstaff.

John Loy, one of the early settlers, was instrumental in initiating this effort. The road was to follow the cattle trail as it headed north of Oak Creek. The roadbed was cut through the rocks almost entirely by hand. Wages were $1.00 per day, and that was not for a measly 8 hour day! Contrary to common belief, T.C. Schnebly had little or nothing to do with the actual construction of Schnebly Hill Road. T.C. did not arrive in this area until October, 1901. His brother, Ellsworth, already living here, was the owner of an 80 acre farm near present day Tlaquepaque. He had purchased the land from the Frank Owenbys, who had homesteaded the land. Ellsworth had secured pledges totaling $300 from businessmen in Coconino County to cover some of the cost of building the road. All but one of those investors reneged on their pledges, and a total of $10 was actually collected. J.J. Thompson had put together a crew and they worked on the road for several weeks. They never got a dime of the money. The road actually opened in 1902, and it was the main "highway" to Flagstaff for several years.

So how and why did the Munds Trail become the Schnebly Hill Road? It was pretty much from common usage. T.C. Schnebly and his wife Sedona had their home (our first functioning bed and breakfast) located near the base of the road (near present day Los Abrigados). Their home was a ten room, two story building called the Schnebly Hotel. (Eventually the post office called "Sedona" would be located in the hotel.) Folks heading down to this area from Flagstaff started calling the road "Schnebly Hill Road" because it led down the mountain right to the Schnebly Hotel where many of them would stay. You must admit this was pretty good public relations for the hotel. The hotel functioned until the Schneblys left Arizona in 1905 (they returned about 1931). The building was destroyed in a fire in 1918.

It was not until 1939 when Hwy.89A through Oak Creek Canyon was paved that the Schnebly Hill Road became a secondary route to Flagstaff. 89A had been built in a piecemeal fashion over the years from 1913 to 1939. The paving of that road sounded the death knell for the first road to Flagstaff. Once the Forest Service took over the maintenance of Schnebly Hill Road it was doomed by "benign neglect." Today that early marvel of highway development, constructed by pick and shovel, is suitable only for those daring folks in their four wheel drive vehicles.

RED ROCK – The Place

What is Red Rock? Do you have any idea where it is? Did you know that Red Rock was a thriving settlement here years before Sedona became Sedona? Red Rock is that area encompassed by the Dumas Ranch, the Schuerman Ranch, the Chavez Ranch and Red Rock Crossing. For those folks who recognize only the name Red Rock Crossing, you reach the area by taking 89A west out of Sedona to Upper Red Rock Loop Road, then follow the Loop Road south as it meanders down toward the creek. Don't make the turn to go to Crescent Moon Park (Chavez Ranch Road), but keep following the Loop Road. On your right you will pass the old Pioneer Cemetery, where a number of the old timers are buried, and on your left you might catch a peek of the remnants of the old Red Rock School House. What fun to find out that Sedona was not always the center of this Red Rock paradise we call home, but that the settlement of Red Rock provided its residents with the comfort and culture missing from their lives in this beautiful but harsh land.

Henry Schuerman and his wife Doretta were the first real settlers of Red Rock. When they arrived in 1885, there were barely discernible trails, much less roads. Henry had taken title to 160 acres on lower Oak Creek in payment of a $500 debt owed by Tom Carrol, who had earlier homesteaded land in what is now West Sedona. They bought a wagon and team, a stock of groceries, hired a driver, and headed out on a five day journey from Prescott to their newly acquired farm on the creek. When they arrived at their wilderness holdings, they found only a ramshackle cabin (whose cabin is a mystery) and the remains of an Indian irrigation ditch, a remembrance left by early Native Americans who also found this Red Rock land inviting. It was beautiful country, and it was remote – so remote that they couldn't give the place away. So what did they do? They stayed and put down roots, eventually acquiring even more land through the Homestead Act.

Other families came and settled in the same area. It was good land, close to water, land that was able to support orchards and vineyards, as well as the more mundane farm crops. A few families settled on farms and ranches on the southeast side of the Creek near the area known more generally as Big Park. Children were born, families were growing, and a community was being formed.

By 1890, the children of those growing families were approaching the age when they were ready to learn reading and writing and numbers, at the least. Education was a primary priority to these early settlers. A few of them may have been illiterate, but many were well versed in literature, mathematics, and music. They wanted the same opportunity to learn for their children in the Red Rock area. Henry Schuerman was determined that the children, including his own growing family, would be able to attend a school that was convenient for them. He was the driving force in petitioning for a school. Schuerman gave the land and offered to donate the building of the structure. The newly formed school board hired a teacher, and the school was opened in the fall of 1891.

After just a few years, the growing population shifted, and more children were living on the northwest side of Oak Creek as it looped through the Schuerman property. Henry donated more land, this time on the west side of his property, and the lumber needed to build the new school. That school, still only one room — but larger, was known as Red Rock School District No. 27. When Oak Creek flooded, as it did at least annually, the children from the east side/Big Park spent nights with families on the west side. Families who lived up in Oak Creek Canyon would move to Red Rock during the winter so their children could attend school. Laura Purtyman McBride was born in a tent at Red Rock because her mother, Clara Thompson Purtyman, had taken Laura's older sister to school there. Clara Purtyman herself had been a student in the first class of the school in 1891. The 1897 school records indicate that fourteen children were in attendance, including youngsters from the Thompson, Chavez, Huckaby, James, and Schuerman families.

The first school teacher, Miss Minnie Maxwell, taught arithmetic, reading, language, spelling, geography, and "copy-books" (what we called penmanship). The teacher would room and board at the home of one of the pupils. The Henry Schuermans often offered their hospitality to the current teacher. The school remained a one room schoolhouse throughout its existence. Although an addition constructed of rock was built by the WPA in the 1930s, it was mainly a stage for plays and pageants. The school continued until the end of the 1946-47 school year. It died because its enrollment shrunk. Arizona law required that there be at least eight students in order to have a viable school. After that school year, there would be fewer than eight students. The last teacher at Red Rock School was Ruth Jordan, wife of Walter Jordan. Two of the students were Walter Jordan, Jr. and his sister Ruth. (The Jordan farm in Uptown Sedona is now the site of the Sedona Heritage Museum and is on the National Register of Historic Buildings.)

The Red Rock Cemetery, also known as the Pioneer Cemetery, was established by Henry Schuerman to bury his daughter, Clara, who died when she was four years old. If you walk through the cemetery, now under the guardianship of the Sedona Historical Society, you will recognize names of some of the early settlers in the area.

As its neighbor to the east has grown and become known world wide, Red Rock, like Brigadoon, has gone to sleep, remembered only by the descendants of those who once lived and thrived there, but remaining unknown to the thousands of recent arrivals to this beautiful Red Rock country.

(As always, my thanks and acknowledgments to the Sedona Historical Society and its wonderful archives that make this research easy as well as fun.)

THE SAND SCULPTURES

Were you here when the sand sculptures were part of the fascination of Oak Creek Canyon? When David and I were first coming to Sedona to vacation (before we got Red Rock Fever) we always looked forward to the stunning sand sculptures along the east side of 89A through the Canyon (just north of mileage marker 378). Tourist buses would stop there regularly. And then they were gone! Created by artist Ted Conibear (supposedly using a teaspoon!) in the late 1960s, the statues served as a landmark for people driving through the canyon. Folks would give directions using the statues as a focus point, i.e. the house is two blocks from the statues. But in late 1986 the sculptures were discovered by a different breed...vandals. On two different nights the heads of Christ in the Garden and the apostles at the Last Supper were shattered.

Ted Conibear, the sculptor, had been creating religious sand sculptures for over 60 years. (He died in 1994 at the age of 88.) Conibear made a career of creating religious sand sculptures at fairs and other national gatherings. His first Last Supper was created in downtown Los Angeles in 1939. The Oak Creek Last Supper was his tenth and last. His most famous works were displayed at Bible Land in Temecula, California. None of them currently exist. Time, wind erosion, and lack of maintenance contributed to the loss of the Bible Land sculptures. But it was vandals who destroyed the Oak Creek sculptures.

The land the sculptures sat on was owned by a Phoenix business man who thought the statues were out of place, even though they were in place before he bought the land in 1982. His rationale was that the canyon was supposed to be a natural place, but he had never seen anywhere where God created sand sculptures. The land purchase did bring him income as he charged Conibear $500 per month to display his work. Coconino County officials estimated that about $2000 per month came in donations from tourists to Conibear, although that figure was disputed.

There was squabbling going on between the property owner who wanted to build a ten room retreat on the land and Mr. Conibear who wanted the sculptures left intact. Conibear repaired the 1986 damage, but the further destruction just a few years later was too much. By the mid 1990s it was gone. Eventually the rubble of what had been stunning artwork was removed by the Highway Department. The ten room retreat was never built.

Jesus Sand Sculpture
Photo courtesy of Cindy Rovey

SCHNEBLY HILL ROAD – WHAT HAPPENED?!

Schnebly Hill Road originated as a shortcut between the summer range for cattle near Flagstaff and the winter range in the Verde Valley. William Munds (of Munds Park fame) had homesteaded land both in the Verde Valley and above the Rim outside of Flagstaff. The route to move his cattle from winter to summer grazing meant heading south, then east, and then north. Necessity being the mother of invention, Munds hacked a cattle trail up the east wall of Oak Creek Canyon which was 35 miles-- and 2 days-- shorter than the old route between the grazing ranges.

The cattle trail was fine for ranching, but as more settlers arrived in the Sedona area they were looking for a quicker way to get themselves and their wagons up to Flagstaff. In 1896, John Loy was instrumental in the growth of a road from the Mund cattle trail. With volunteers, pick axes, shovels, and black powder, in five years they constructed the Verde Cut-Off Road.

In 1902 the Coconino County Board of Supervisors awarded a $600 contract to J.J. Thompson, a Civil War veteran on the Confederate side, to improve this road. The men worked 12 hour days at $1.00 per day (no minimum wage back then). In six months time the new "Munds Road" was completed. Now, like the cattle, the settlers could get from Sedona to Flagstaff in only two days. Because T.C. Schnebly had built a home near the end of the road, which his wife, Sedona, had turned into an inn, Munds Road took on the name of Schnebly Hill Road. The total cost of this pioneer highway - $1800.00!

Sedonans used this as their primary route to Flagstaff until the dirt road through Oak Creek Canyon was completed in 1914. Schnebly Hill Road was never paved, but it was reengineered in 1930. People still used the road, especially when the movie companies included awesome shots of the Canyon from the road. Although travel on it was minimal, the road was maintained to some extent. Then, in 1950, folks were outraged to find that that the road was barricaded. Coconino County, in its infinite wisdom, denied owning it and would not maintain it. The citizens refused to take that without a fight. Record review showed that all county legal requirements had been met, county funds ($1800.00) had been expended, and the county did, indeed, own it.

The road continued to be sparsely used, but was negotiable. However, the road is now in the hands of the Forest Service, and is a part of the Mund's Mountain Wilderness Area. Today, you will take the life of your vehicle in hand if you try to drive from Sedona to Flagstaff on the road. I can still remember that my husband and I drove the road in a low slung sports car — without any problem — as recently as 1994. Wow! Time does fly.

Photo courtesy of D.L.Benore

SCHOOLMARMS IN YAVAPAI COUNTY

Teaching school in the early part of the 20th century took a special talent and fortitude. Most of the teachers were miles from their homes and families. Many were young women, some with college degrees and some without high school diplomas. She was pretty much isolated in the rural area or small town that housed a one or two room school. But teaching school provided one of the few respectable jobs for a single woman. If a woman married, she probably lost her job as a teacher...unless she became a widow.

Elsie Hayes, a young woman in her mid-twenties, made her way from Long Beach, California to Cornville, AZ in 1913. The journey was itself an education. The position had been arranged by the California Teachers' Agency. She and her companion and fellow teacher had traveled by the Santa Fe train to near Prescott via the narrow-gauge United Verde and Pacific Railroad into Jerome. From there a stagecoach would take them to Cornville.

Sedona School
Photo courtesy of Sedona Historical Society

Elsie was pretty tough, so the lack of electricity or running water was not a problem. There was nothing in Cornville but a small post office that served as the only store. Otherwise, there were ranches spread around which included about 25 families. This school did have 2 rooms. The teachers boarded with one of the families until a shed could be set up to house the two women. Elsie taught the first 5 grades; her co-teacher taught the other 3. Textbooks were very limited and had to be shared, although the pupils did have slates to write on. Depending on the weather, she could have as few as 2 pupils or as many as 18. Though books were limited, Elsie read to her pupils: poetry, literature, history, geography and basic math. One of the first grade lessons was "dramatization." This teacher made such an impression on her students that 70 years later (after she taught only 1 year in Cornville) the students remembered her. (Source: "Very Lovingly Yours, Elsie". Barbara Anne Waite)

Edith Croxen (nee Lamport) was a schoolmarm in Sedona from 1914 through 1916. She had 33 pupils, grades 1-8, in a one room schoolhouse that stood on the playground of a later Sedona school. The holiday season of 1915-16 was the winter of the deep snow. After the big Christmas party at the school, Edith planned to spend the holidays with her parents in Flagstaff. In order to get there, she had to get from Sedona to Clarkdale by horseback, get on the train in Clarkdale to go to Drake and Ashfork, and thence to Flagstaff. While she was in Flag, the snows came down...for three days, leaving sixty-four inches of the white stuff on level ground. The whole Verde Valley was covered with at least two feet of snow. This made for an exciting trip to get back to open the school after the holiday. Her Sedona experience did prepare Edith for her future. She married Fred Croxen, a National Forest Ranger, and followed him throughout his postings in Arizona. She taught school wherever he went, including his years as a Border Patrolman in Hereford, Arizona, and as Law and Order Director on the Navajo Reservation in Window Rock. This Yavapai County schoolmarm was prepared for an exciting life.

SEDONA-WHAT'S IN A NAME?

Sedona Arabella Miller was born in February, 1877, into the family of a prosperous landowner in Gorin, Missouri. She was one of ten children. The Miller children were well educated. In addition to reading, writing and arithmetic, they learned French, German, elocution, and music. Her mother was a genteel, refined lady, which is why in a family of Minnies, Noahs, Johnnys, etc., Mrs. Miller decided she wanted a prettier name for her daughter with big brown eyes. She made up the name because she liked the way it sounded. No, contrary to what people may believe, the name is not French, Spanish, Native American, or biblical (although there is a Sidonia in the Old Testament) . It was pretty much a product of Mrs. Miller's imagination.

When Sedona was in her late teens she met and fell in love with a Gorin merchant, T. C. (Theodore Carl) Schnebly, who was eight years older than Sedona. The match was not approved of by the Millers. First of all, the Millers were Methodists, and T.C. was a "predestination Presbyterian," and second, Mr. Miller thought T.C. was a dreamer, a man who would never amount to anything. According to family legend, when Sedona married T.C. on her 20th birthday, she was struck from her father's will.

T.C.'s brother, Dorsey Ellsworth, was living in the red rock country that would become Sedona. He wrote to his brother extolling the delights of this area. T.C. was convinced. He turned over his share of the Gorin hardware business to his brothers, and moved his young family to the Arizona Territory.

T.C. left first, and two weeks later Sedona with the two children, Ellsworth, age 3, and Pearl, almost 2, followed, along with a railroad car loaded with their possessions. They traveled by rail to Jerome, and then by wagon to the 80 acres T.C. had purchased from Frank Owenby. That 80 acres today includes Tlaquepaque, Los Abrigados, and all the development between Portal Lane and the old ranger station. T.C. hired men who helped build an eleven room, two story home—the first functioning bed and breakfast in Sedona. Their guests eventually included travelers heading to Jerome, gentlemen on fishing trips up Oak Creek Canyon, and tubercular patients headed West to a gentler climate.

The young Mr. Schnebly was, indeed, a wheeler-dealer. He planted orchards and vegetables which he marketed up in Flagstaff. He brought back staples, mail, and visitors from his forays up to Flag. Some neighbors and boarders complained about the irregular mail service, so T.C. decided that a post office was in order, and he would be the first postmaster. The postal authorities agreed. However, a name was required for the post office. His first two suggestions—Schnebly Station and Oak Creek Crossing were too long to fit in with "Arizona Territory" on the cancellation stamp. His brother said "Why not call it after Dona?" Washington agreed, and on June 26, 1902, the post office called Sedona opened in the front room of the family home.

The Schneblys enjoyed a relatively comfortable and prosperous life. In 1903 another daughter, Genevieve, was born. In 1904 T.C. helped facilitate a grant from Coconino County to finish what would become known as Schnebly Hill Road between Sedona and Flagstaff.

In 1905, tragedy struck. Sedona, with little Genevieve on her lap, and 5 year old Pearl and 7 year old Ellsworth on their cow ponies, were rounding up cattle one evening. The children had a treasure trove of arrowheads, and Pearl spotted another. She looped the reins around her neck while she bent down to add it to her collection. At that instant a cow began to stray, the trained cow pony leaped to bring it back, Pearl fell off the pony, the pony panicked, and ran. By the time Sedona and Ellsworth caught the pony, little Pearl was dead. Sedona, understandably, fell into a deep depression. The local doctor, who was pretty savvy for the time, told T.C. to "move her or lose her."

The Schneblys left Sedona. They moved back to Missouri for some years and eventually to eastern Colorado. They had three more children. T.C. in a way fulfilled his father-in-law's prophecy. He failed in business and in ranching, not usually his fault. At his ranch in Boyero, Colorado, in one season his herd developed anthrax and had to be destroyed, and his crops were wiped out by a hailstorm. They came back to Sedona with their two youngest daughters who were teenagers.

T.C. worked for Walter Jordan in the orchard, and since her own daughters didn't need her as much, Sedona worked for the Jordans, helping to raise the three Jordan children and keeping house for Ruth Jordan. The Jordans still refer to her as Aunt Dona.

Sedona was deeply involved in her family, friends, the town named for her, and especially the Wayside Chapel. She was instrumental in bringing it into being. Sedona died in 1950, and T.C. died in 1954.

THE FIRST LADY OF SEDONA

Laura Purtymun McBride is recognized by those who knew her, or know anything about her, as the First Lady of Sedona. She embodies the history of the quiet hamlet that became world-famous Sedona. She was also multi-talented. Laura was a junk collector, an avant-garde artist, an environmentalist before it became fashionable, a story teller and a talented writer. All this in one leggy, lanky lady!

Laura was born in Oak Creek Canyon in 1910. Her forbears included J.J. Thompson (the original Anglo settler in Oak Creek Canyon), the legendary Bear Howard, and most immediately Clara Thompson and Albert Purtymun. She often bemoaned the fact that her sisters were small and delicate, but she took after the men in her family, tall and rangy.

From the time she was a young child, Laura was fascinated with the history of her family as well as the other pioneers in the area. She was a good listener and absorbed the stories and lore of the early Red Rock Country. Laura's education was interesting, to say the least. She attended the one-room school in Oak Creek Canyon as well as Red Rock School (near Red Rock Crossing). But when she was thirteen, the family embarked on a trip that equaled a Master's Degree in survival.

Laura's parents had decided to visit Grandpa Purtymun in California. Unfortunately, the border between California and Arizona was closed because of an outbreak of hoof and mouth disease. So the Purtymun clan packed everything they owned into three old Model T Fords and headed to California via New Mexico, Colorado, Utah, Idaho, Oregon, and finally to California. They had very little money, so they worked their way on their journey. (See photo of Laura as young teen.) Fifty-five years later, Laura put it all together in a classic book TRAVELING BY TIN LIZZIE. If you haven't read it, you are missing a real treat..."The Grapes of Wrath" with a happy ending (available at the Heritage Museum and at Amazon.)

Laura as a teenager with siblings

When she was 21 she married Ray McBride. The copper smelter in Clarkdale closed in the late 1930s, and he lost his job. The McBrides moved up to the Thompson property in Oak Creek Canyon. Ray put his talents to work building a home from scrap lumber and tin. And Laura found an outlet for her creativity. She built walls around the property. And the walls were embedded with "junk" she had collected...much of which had sentimental value to her and others. After the walls were built, she created walking paths and rock art. She even built a gold fish pond with a waterfall. She often said that being a junk collector was great fun.

Laura was a living encyclopedia on any and everything about Oak Creek Canyon and the Red Rock Country. Any questions you had, she could answer. She was the "go-to" interviewee by journalists, magazine writers, and even commercial videographers. She never turned anyone down. Her love of the history of the area fostered her enthusiasm to help found the Sedona Historical Society, which gave birth to the Sedona Heritage Museum, one of the gems of greater Sedona. Laura died in 1994, active and energetic to the end.

WHAT OR WHO IS SHARLOT HALL?

When I first heard of Sharlot Hall a dozen or more years ago, I assumed it was the name of another of those interesting pioneer type museums indigenous to many of the towns in Arizona. And who was this "Sharlot" person that the hall was named for? It didn't take too long (or very much research) to realize that Sharlot Hall was a person, a woman who could be described as a renaissance woman in Arizona'a history. She was a poet, a writer, a champion of statehood, and a preservationist long before it became a popular pastime.

Sharlot was born in Kansas in 1870, but moved with her family to the Arizona Territory in 1881. Settling near Dewey in Yavapai County, she was educated in public schools in Dewey and Prescott.

Sharlot Hall was a prolific writer, having sold her first story — the retelling of a Hopi myth — at age 20 to a children's magazine for the munificent sum of $4.00. Actually, not bad money in 1890 for an unknown writer. In her lifetime, she went on to publish over 500 articles, stories and poems, as well as ten books.

Her love of Arizona is what defined her. As a young girl and later as a young woman, she wandered over the deserts and mountains of the Territory, studying the Native Americans, the history and geology of the Southwest, and collecting relics and specimens for archeological and historical purposes when ladies did not do those things. She fought to preserve and publicize Arizona's heritage. Sharlot was an outdoorswoman. She expressed it beautifully when she wrote, "I'm glad, so glad that God let me be an outdoor woman and love the big things. I couldn't be a tame house cat woman...but God meant women to joy in his great clean beautiful world...he lets me see some of it not through a window pane."

In 1905 Congress proposed to admit the Arizona and New Mexico Territories as a single state. Sharlot wrote the epic poem "Arizona," which mocked the proposal, making a case for Arizona as an independent state. She gave a copy of the poem to every member of Congress. She served as the official State Historian for 3 years, and was titled Poet Laureate of Arizona. When Calvin Coolidge was elected president in 1924, Sharlot was one of the three Republican electors pledged to support him. She was named to carry the three electoral votes to Washington. She worried that she had no wardrobe grand enough, so the Arizona Industrial Congress commissioned an overdress of copper mesh links, an apt advertisement for the Copper State.

In 1928, her pet project came to fruition. The old Governor's Mansion opened as a museum. That one building museum is now part of the nine building campus known as the Sharlot Hall Museum. Sharlot died in 1943 and was one of the first inductees to the Women's Hall of Fame. The next time you travel to Prescott, take an hour or two and step into Arizona's days of yore.

Copper link dress on display at Sharlot Hall Museum

A GRANDSON OF THE PIONEERS

This is the tale of a grandson of Red Rock pioneers. You have heard about Heinrich and Doretta Schuerman who emigrated from Prussia to Red Rock Country via Prescott in 1880. They begat several children, including a daughter Frieda. William Loy was the son of Samuel and Jane Loy who had settled in the Verde Valley in 1876. William married Nellie and they begat Myron. Frieda Schuerman and Myron Loy married in 1924 and begat Sherman Adelbert Loy who was born in 1926 and Martha Joan who was born 6 years later. Sherman's DNA and bloodline were pure Red Rock Country.

Sherman was born in Cornville, and actually lived the first two years of his life at Crescent Moon Ranch at Red Rock Crossing. He went to school at Red Rock School which was founded by his grandfather Schuerman in 1891. He went on to Sedona School before graduating from Clarkdale High School in 1944. The army came looking for young men, and Sherman was drafted, eventually ending up in the Pacific Islands.

Sherman Loy
Photo Courtesy Sedona
Historical Society

After six years he came home and went to work for a cattle outfit that provided stunt horses for the movie business. Sherman's job was to sleep in the barn with them to make sure nothing happened. According to him, he was paid pretty well for it and was able to enroll in college under the G.I. Bill of Rights. He also enrolled in a reserve officer program. That was tempting because it paid him an additional $30.00 per month. Before he was able to complete his degree Sherman was called into the Korean Conflict. He spent the next 18 years specializing in artillery and travelling all over the world. He managed to finish his degree in 1963 and then was sent on to Vietnam in 1967. According to Sherman, "I got there during a hot period of time." After that service he was stationed stateside to begin transitioning to civilian life, retiring as a major. But Oklahoma didn't cut it , he headed back to the lure of Red Rock Country.

Let's face it. He was born with Red Rock Fever. Sherman spent 10 years working for a security company and did some ranching on the side. Like so many of the early settlers here, education was of paramount importance. He served a decade on the district school board, chairman for 4 years. According to Sherman, he finally ticked off enough people that he lost his last election by 14 votes. "I have a propensity for popping off sometimes." Sherman was a crusty, cantankerous old curmudgeon who enjoyed every minute of being one. He either liked you or he didn't...and there wasn't much you could about that.

Historical preservation became his passion. Anthropology and archaeology provided the foundation for his dedication to preserving the past. He was involved with the Friends of the Forest, Arizona Site Steward Program, was active in the Verde Valley Archaeology Society, and the Sedona Historical Society as historian and board member. He put his time and talent where his heart was. And Red Rock Country is richer for it. Sherman Loy died in May, 2011. I miss him.

THE STOPWATCH GANG

Everyone's heard of the "Over the Hill Gang," a 1969 western movie starring Pat O'Brien and Walter Brennan. And who doesn't recall the exploits of Butch Cassidy and the "Hole in the Wall Gang" up there in Wyoming? But have you ever heard of the Stopwatch Gang, whose "hole in the wall" was right here in Oak Creek Canyon in days of recent yore?

The Stopwatch Gang was made up of three affable Canadians who, in the 1970s and 1980s, were the most successful bank robbers in the United States. In the course of their crime career, they were purported to have stolen more than $15 million dollars. They still hold the record for being the most successful bank robbers in North American history. In one job in San Diego, they made off with $283,000 in cash. Back home in Ottawa, they stole $750,000 in gold bars . . . and their hideaway was in our own beloved Oak Creek Canyon.

The mastermind was Patrick (Paddy) Mitchell – an average suburban family man. Steven Reid was a former A-student and athletic star. Lionel Wright was a newspaper office boy. A rather unpretentious group who led law enforcement and the FBI on a merry chase for almost two decades as they robbed an estimated 100 banks.

Their modus operandi included Paddy using a stopwatch on his neck during the robbery to make sure it took no longer than 2 minutes from start to finish. They would use diversions, i.e. calling in bomb threats to other parts of town to mislead the police. They were occasionally arrested, but managed to escape much like the old Keystone Kops.

Their safe haven was Oak Creek Canyon. There they lived in a secluded home in the 1980s while they were on the FBI's most wanted list. They made many friends here. Reid played bridge regularly with a Coconino County Deputy Sheriff and his wife. The guys used to come into Sedona to shop and to launder some of the money by making purchases and swapping stolen bills for untraceable bills. They had close friends in Sedona who were shocked when they found out, but stood by them. They really liked the men. They just happened to rob banks for a living.

Eventually all were caught and convicted. The FBI agent Greg Weston wrote a great book about them — "The Stopwatch Gang" — and a local Sedona film group, All of the Above Productions, LLC, is in the process of chronicling their escapades. Paddy died in 2007. Reid became a noted author. Wright became an accountant with the Department of Corrections in Canada.

And now you know something about the Stopwatch Gang, the most famous unknown gang who hid away in Oak Creek Canyon!

SI BIRCH

What's in a name? You may have noticed that SR89A through West Sedona is named the Si Birch Memorial Highway. There are road signs on 89A at Upper Red Rock Loop Road and just west of the double round-about in West Sedona delineating that portion of the roadway in memory of him. If you frequent the main branch of the Sedona Library you may have seen the name Si Birch Community Room spelled out above the large meeting room. There is another memorial plaque at the Sedona Medical Center. Interesting. But who was Si Birch?

It took some searching to discover the background of this man. Fortunately, there is archival material at the Sedona Historical Society.

Like most of the citizens of Sedona, Si Birch was a transplant. He was born in Ohio in 1917 and spent six years in the army during World War II. After that war he immigrated west to California and spent 27 years working for the City of Los Angeles in the Department of Public Works.

Mr. Birch retired to Sedona (a community of about 2000) in 1975 and became involved with the growing pains of a town in development. He was not a man who took to retirement easily and soon had his fingers in many pies. He was a man whose major talent was to get others excited about creating the infrastructure needed to make Sedona develop. He himself admitted in a 1989 interview that he seemed to get things done through other people. "I don't really do that much myself." He seemed to be the catalyst that helped bring about the first Arizona scenic road designations for Oak Creek Canyon and Hwy. 179 (many years before the more prestigious Federal designation of SR179 as an All American Road). Other groups he was involved with produced the brown and cream street signs, the rustic guard rail systems, street and house numbering, and the first official street map for the newly incorporated (1988) Sedona. He was president of the Sedona Healthcare Services (the first licensed free standing clinic created to support the one doctor--that's right ONE) in Sedona. In 1988 he was named as the first Citizen of the Year by the Red Rock News, and in 1992 he began a four year term as a city council member.

Some of the other memberships he held included the Sedona Medical Center Advisory Committee, Keep Sedona Beautiful, Sedona-Coconino Taxpayers' Association, Sedona Public Library board, Adult Community Center, Red Rock High School Booster Club, Masonic Lodge, and the Sedona School District site committee. He also played in the Sedona Hometown Band for 18 years. It makes me wonder...did he ever spend any time at home?

Si Birch died in 1998. Shortly thereafter 89A was designated as the Si Birch Memorial Highway. The community room at the library was named for him when the family made a generous donation to that facility. It is ironic that so many people driving along the Si Birch Memorial Highway in West Sedona have no idea who Si Birch was. *Sic transit gloria*...loosely translated "fame is fleeting."

THE MOVIES AND RED ROCK COUNTRY

Hooray for Hollywood! Or maybe not. What made Sedona and Big Park grow...pure and simple...they were discovered by the folks in Tinseltown. And the rest is history.

As early as 1923, the first movie, a silent film "Call of the Canyon" starring Richard Dix (remember him?) was filmed up in Oak Creek Canyon. It took place at West Fork where Zane Grey, author of the book and screenwriter of the movie, had been inspired to write the novel. The timing — weatherwise — was a fiasco. A raging storm, flooding in the canyon, and the washout of the primitive road forced the cast and crew to be hauled up to Flagstaff for safety's sake. The producer swore that the area was not meant for movies.

However, seven years later, another book by Zane Grey, "Last of the Duanes," was successfully made into a movie, and the rush was on. By the time the boom ended in the early 1970s, at least 57 complete pictures were filmed here, with another 40 that were partially filmed in Red Rock Country. Some were really great. Some were pretty good, and some were really bad. The John Wayne westerns were classics. Henry Fonda starred in the honest to goodness western "Firecreek," and with Glenn Ford had a delightful romp in the "Rounders," a bittersweet comedy about two aging cowboys who had outlived their time in history. This was filmed in Big Park before the Village existed. One of the very worst starred Elvis Presley. It was called "Stay Away, Joe," and people stayed away in droves. Mr. Presley stayed on the Las Vegas stage for the most part after that one.

The movies brought economic stability, if not prosperity, to Red Rock Country. Cash money came into the area. Locals found work as extras, stunt doubles and set builders. When the films were shown throughout the nation, they brought artists and artisans who wanted to soak up the beauty and mystical appeal of this country. Later came the tourists (especially after World War II when gasoline was available for automobile travel) with their particular needs: hotels, restaurants, galleries, guided tours, and the ubiquitous souvenir shops. Many of the tourists eventually became residents.

For good or for bad, the movies were instrumental in making Sedona and Red Rock Country what it is today. And the beauty of this country still reaches those thousands of people who may never actually travel here, but who can get a glimpse of the awesome red rocks through Hollywood and film. Aren't we fortunate? We live here.

WHERE DID THEY GO TO SCHOOL?

Where and how did youngsters get any formal education when there were only a handful of people living in the area? Schooling in the Big Park basin was particularly hard to come by. There were fewer homesteaders here than had settled in what would become Sedona and Oak Creek Canyon. And although there was a school up in the Canyon in the early 1890s, it was too far for youngsters in Big Park.

In 1891 Henry Schuerman was the driving force in getting a school opened in the settlement of Red Rock, just across Oak Creek from Big Park. As the population of Red Rock and Big Park increased, a larger school was needed (still one room, but a larger room). Through Mr. Schuerman's donation of his land and the lumber needed for the physical building, the new school, known as Red Rock School District No. 27, became a reality. Children from Big Park crossed Oak Creek to attend class. It was certainly the closest educational facility for them. When Oak Creek flooded, as it was wont to do at least on an annual basis, the Big Park youngsters would spend those nights with Red Rock families.

Although a Mr. Harper, a homesteader east of today's Verde Valley School Road, is thought to have built the first school on the east side of Oak Creek, the first recorded school in Big Park was built in the early 1920s. It served as a community center as well as a school for the homesteading families of that era. Everyone pitched in — much like an old fashioned barn raising — to build a 20x40 foot building. It had a tin roof to catch rain and drain it into a storage cistern to be used by the students and the teacher. (No one in Big Park had a well in those days.) There was no insulation, of course, so the building was close to being an oven in the spring and fall, and it was a huge ice box in the winter.

According to an article written by Kel Fox, the original school (ca. 1927) was located very close to the red rocks on the extreme west end of the Oakcreek Country Club golf course. In the late 1930s the school was moved to a spot just behind what is now the Big Park post office. But the school population was diminishing. Arizona law required a minimum of 8 students to have a "legal" school. In fact, according to Mr. Fox, a school board member, he remembers hiring a teacher because she would bring an extra student — her daughter — to make the required total of eight.

The farmers and small ranchers were not making it. The land had not yet been discovered by the developers. The school closed in 1941 — no students. The district was abolished by the school superintendent. The old school building stood for many years, forlorn and abandoned. It was torn down in the 1960s by the original developers of the Village of Oak Creek. So much for historic preservation!

BIG PARK COMMUNITY SCHOOL REBORN

What a difference forty years makes! When a lack of students forced the closure of Big Park School in 1941, none of the residents dreamed that in four short decades there would be a demand for a local school to serve the growing population in the Village of Oak Creek/Big Park. The original school was a community effort in the fullest sense of the term. The locals contributed the building materials as well as the labor. Included in the project was a small cabin for the teacher. And it didn't cost the taxpayers a cent. In the late 1930s the school was moved to a spot behind what would become Fanny Gulick's ranch house. There is a wonderful photo showing the isolation of the old school building near SR 179 in the Pro Shop of the Oakcreek Country Club.

By the 1980s, it became apparent that a school was needed in the Village. The development of the Village of Oak Creek, along with the smaller developments of Pine Valley, Pinion Woods, Oak Creek Estates, etc. brought families with young children into the area. The new locals wanted a local school. Schools in Sedona were filled with children from Sedona and busing was a hassle.

Times had changed, though, and it was no longer simply a matter of residents getting together with materials and labor to build a school. It was 1987 and there was now a school district. Studies were needed to determine the viability of a school in the area. The Big Park Land Use Advisory Committee had to approve any proposed site. The parks, recreation and schools subcommittee came up with a suggested site. Its choice for a school and park for the Village of Oak Creek was 200 acres of National Forest land off Jack's Canyon Road near Lee Mountain Road. Yavapai

County was not comfortable with that choice. It saw potential problems with the heavy traffic load at the site. The county suggested that a location closer to the highway would be more feasible.

Big Park School cira 1930

By the early 1990s most of the hurdles had been jumped. The current location along Verde Valley School Road was approved. There were complaints from some of the neighbors of the school who objected to having any school in the area. They were the folks who wanted this to be another Sun City — no kids, just older adults. Fortunately, they were in the minority. Clearing work on Big Park

Community School started in August 1993, with completion to be accomplished in one year.

Community is part of the official name of the school. It has a strong parent teacher organization and great community support. For the past several years it has been noted as one of the outstanding elementary schools in the state, with families wanting to get their children enrolled. Quite a difference from the lonely little schoolhouse that had to be abandoned for lack of students in 1941.

THOSE WERE THE DAYS...

Back in 1876, Jim Thompson took a job as packer and night herder for military mules while the army was looking for Indians. After the evening meal, Jim drove the mules out of sight of the camp. He built a small fire and lay down to take a nap. Unbeknownst to him, some cartridges fell out of his pocket near the fire. At daybreak he woke up cold, raked the charred sticks into the embers to rekindle the fire. A couple of the cartridges were raked into the fire and exploded. He quickly got the mules back into camp where the guard asked if he heard shots. He said he heard them, but saw no one. The soldiers searched, but found no Indians.

Old "Bear" Howard came to Sedona with the Purtyman family about 1880. However, he did not travel with them during the day. He had broken out of jail in California so he avoided the main trail during daylight hours. Bear would come to the Purtyman camp only at night when he was "short of grub." The Purtymans did not travel with a wagon train. They made the trek from California by themselves, just Mr. and Mrs. Purtyman (she was Howard's daughter) and the two Purtyman children. They ran into the aftermath of an Indian raid along the Colorado River, and were brought into safety in Arizona by some soldiers. The Purtymans eventually homesteaded in Oak Creek Canyon. Old Grandpa Bear Howard was a bear hunter and killed a lot of bears. He would butcher them, take them up to Flagstaff where the meat was sold over the block in butcher shops, much as pork and beef.

Edith Croxen was a schoolmarm in Sedona during the years 1915-1916, the winter of the deep snow. After the big Christmas party at the school, she planned to spend the holidays with her parents up in Flagstaff. In order to get there, she had to get from Sedona to Clarkdale by horseback, get on the train in Clarkdale to go to Drake and Ashfork, and thence to Flagstaff. While she was in Flag, the snows came down…for three days, leaving sixty-four inches of the white stuff on the level ground. The whole Verde Valley was covered with at least two feet of snow. The train track was finally plowed in time for the schoolmarm to make the return trip by train. She got as far as Cottonwood. After taking refuge there for three days, she and a rancher set off in a buckboard for Sedona, but the road was still covered by two feet of snow. They made it to Cornville to the Hearst ranch. After two days, Edith borrowed a saddle horse and rode with the mail man to Sedona. An unforgettable experience.

These stories are a tiny sample of the wonderful stories told by those who lived them. They are captured in "Those Early Days…" which has finally been reprinted after a hiatus of some 30 years. It is available in the gift shop of the Sedona Heritage Museum. The book is a treasure.

TIDBITS OF TRIVIA

Let's ponder some interesting bits of trivia about this beautiful Red Rock Country in which we live.

Keeping track of the various names given to the different rocks, hamlets, settlements and sections of the region is like trying to solve a jigsaw puzzle where the pieces have a tendency to change shape.

Sedona was originally known as Upper Oak Creek, then as Camp Garden, before the post office was called Sedona in 1902. It wasn't until 1988 that the area was officially incorporated as "Sedona."

Why did it get the name Camp Garden? The area of Sedona was used by the officers of Camp Verde for R & R (rest and recreation) in the latter part of the 19th century.

Because it ran all year long (a rarity for waterways in Arizona), Oak Creek was called "Live Oak Creek" on an Arizona Territorial Map in 1879.

Slide Rock is a very modern name for that area. Until the 1960s, when tourists discovered the creek and found what fun it was to use it as a natural water slide, that part of Oak Creek was known as Oak Creek Falls.

Banjo Bill Campground – This campground and springs up in Oak Creek Canyon was named for Bill Dwyer. He played the banjo, and thus was given the nickname "Banjo Bill." He lived at the springs for about a year in the 1880s. When he moved away, the springs were called Banjo Bill Springs.

What about Snoopy Rock? When you ask folks who have lived here prior to the 1950s, no one had a name for the rock now known as Snoopy. The beloved beagle was born via the pen of Charles Schulz on October 4, 1950. The rock has been here for quite a few centuries. It was generally known as the southwest end of a larger rock known as Camel or Camel Head Rock. (See photo) Nothing terribly clever for the precocious pooch!

Snoopy Rock

The first real school in the area was built in the hamlet of Red Rock, first settled by Henry Schuerman, in 1891. Red Rock was located across Oak Creek from Little Park, just northwest of Big Park. In 1899, a school was built in Oak Creek Canyon midway between the Purtymun and Thompson homesteads. Between the two families, they had enough children to populate the school. The first school in Sedona proper was built in 1914. The first record of a school in Big Park is from the 1920s. It was located close to the red rocks on the west end of today's Oakcreek Country Club golf course. In the late 1930s it was moved.

Jim Thompson, the first Anglo to settle in Oak Creek Canyon, built the original road along Oak Creek from Indian Gardens (his homestead) to Camp Garden/Sedona in the 1880s. He used shovels, picks and dynamite. This road was later washed away in a flood...so Thompson built another road high above the creek. Persistence pays.

"TRAVELING BY TIN LIZZIE"

This year, 2009, is the 100th model year anniversary of the Model T Ford, endearingly known as the "Tin Lizzie." In remembrance, Laura Purtymun McBride wrote of the Tin Lizzie and the migration undertaken by her family in 1924. For no apparent reason, her parents decided to take a trip to California to see Grandpa Purtymun. The border between California and Arizona happened to be closed because of an outbreak of hoof and mouth disease. So they decided that the way to get to California and see some of the country was to go east into New Mexico, north to Colorado, make their way through Utah, Idaho, and Oregon, and finally back down to California. Wandering was in their genetic make up. Clara Purtymun, Laura's mother, was the daughter of J. J. Thompson, who, in his very early teens made his way from Ireland to Galveston, Texas. Clara remembered constant moving both as a girl and later when she was married to Albert Purtymun.

In June of 1924, the Purtymun caravan of three Model Ts started moving on out. The first vehicle, a truck, carried the Purtymuns and the younger children, including eleven year old Laura. The kids sat on the mattresses packed in back. The second vehicle held Laura's sister Erma and her husband. Their car had a small platform behind the cab piled with everything they owned. Bringing up the rear was a stripped down Tin Lizzie belonging to newly weds Kenneth and Della Greenwell, the eldest Purtymun daughter.

What a journey it turned out to be. At the very start Albert got distracted while he was driving, ran off the road, and overturned the car twice. A man with a team of horses pulled them up, and they continued on their way up Oak Creek Canyon. Clara walked up the switchbacks behind the car, carrying her three year old son and a big rock. The rock would be used to chock a wheel in case the motor died and the brakes failed. At the top of the canyon, they headed east on the first leg of their jaunt. Since they had little money, they really had to make do along the way. They picked fruit when they could get work. The men worked in hay fields. They never actually went hungry, but their diet was pretty limited at times. Clara remembered living on black-eyed peas and prunes through most of Idaho. All along the way they picked up used tires that had been tossed along the road by more prosperous drivers.

Purtymun Family
Courtesy of Sedona Historical Society

They were certainly better than what the Purtymuns had. If the "found" tires did not have tubes, the family stuffed them with rags, tied them with baling wire and hoped for the best. When the wires wore out in Oregon, the rags flew out in all directions.

A little over six months later, they arrived in Southern California. All the Purtymuns and all the Model Ts made it. Albert had to borrow fifty dollars from his mother to make the last leg of the journey from California to Arizona, but they all got back with memories that would last a lifetime.

Fifty-five years later, Laura chronicled that journey in a delightful book, "Traveling by Tin Lizzie," ("Grapes of Wrath" with a happy ending), guaranteed to keep you chuckling from beginning to end. The reprint is available at the Sedona Heritage Museum.

GEE – HOW DO YOU PRONOUNCE TLAQUEPAQUE?

Although it looks like it's been around for several centuries, Tlaquepaque (Tuh-lah-kee-pah-kee) is the modern result of one man, Abe Miller, and his dream.

Named after a charming suburb of Guadalajara, Mexico, Mr. Miller attempted to recreate the original arts and crafts village that went back to pre-Hispanic times (!).

Tlaquepaque
Photo courtesy of D. Benore

Abe Miller was a successful Nevada businessman who came to Sedona for vacations in the '60s. At that time (do you remember?) Sedona had one stop light, and much of the land was open range. Abe was a traveler and he loved Mexico, but he fell in love with Sedona—it wasn't even officially a city at that time. The land that captivated him was the creek side property of Harry and Ruby Girard. Two years of gentle persuasion and promises that the sycamores would remain untouched convinced the Girards that their land would be safe in Abe's hands.

Known as "The Art and Soul of Sedona," the village had its birth pangs in 1971 when the stone wall was built along SR-179. (It actually opened in 1973) Abe believed that Sedona was a natural location for a living, thriving arts community. So in order to maintain the integrity of his dream, he kept strict control over the planning, construction, and all the landscaping and continuing maintenance. Bob McIntyre, his architect, was known to be gifted, but unconventional. Abe and his contractor, Bill Herrick, flew in Abe's plane all over Mexico, researching, photographing, and documenting. They bought relics, crafts and artwork, just like a couple of cultural anthropologists at a giant yard sale. Everything from giant carved doors to clay pots were trucked up to Sedona.

Meanwhile, the very unconventional architect hired only amateur artisans for the buildings...self-trained plasterers, "do-it-yourself" stonemasons, etc. Unlike other construction sites, the favorite saying at this one was "Forget the plumb, use the thumb." Everything was eyeballed! The buildings were constructed around existing trees and, as much as possible, methods of construction mirrored those of the old Mexican craftsmen. When construction began, they built an experimental building, just to see what made artistic sense. It would be torn down when the project was completed. But, Abe fell in love with it and could not demolish it. It is now the El Rincon Restaurante Mexicano.

The chapel was Abe's favorite building. He commissioned a 12 foot square painting that included St. Augustine, Pope Pius X, Sts. Bonaventure, Peter, John the

Baptist, and Samuel. He and his wife painted the gold leaf frame that sets off the work. The chapel was meant to be a place of serenity amidst the hustle and bustle of the craft village.

Landscaping was a major challenge. Abe kept his promise to the Girards that the sycamore grove would remain safe. Buildings were designed around the trees at great cost in labor and materials. As the years went on, and the trees grew, you will find limbs merging with roof lines and growing through walls. In fact, inside the Roth jewelry store a tree twists up through the roof. When SR-179 and the bridge at Tlaquepaque were redesigned by ADOT, the design deliberately allowed all the sycamores to remain. Way to go, Abe!

By the way, Tlaquepaque is a word from the Nahuati language—the ancient language of the Aztecs—which means "the best of everything." Appropriate, I would say.

TRIVIA, TALL TALES, AND OTHER LORE

This is an article to address interesting little tidbits of information that would not fill a column, but will make an interesting paragraph. For instance:

Jacks Canyon – According to Albert Thompson's research, the canyon — south and east of the Village of Oak Creek, was named for Jackie Montgomery, a little man who had cattle, but was no cowhand. He used the canyon to move cattle up to Munds Park.

Bugscuffle – That was one of the names given to a portion of Sedona around the old Sedona school. A bunch of cowboys camped at the western portion of Schnebly Hill decided to go down "to the dance at Bugscuffle" (the school). The name stuck.

Slide Rock – That is a name that came about in the 1960s when tourists started coming to the area and began sliding down the creek. Previously it was known as The Falls, according to the Pendley family who homesteaded the place.

Banjo Bill Campground – This campground and springs up in Oak Creek Canyon was named for Bill Dwyer. He played the banjo, and thus was given the nickname "Banjo Bill." He lived at the springs for about a year in the 1880s. When he moved away, the springs were called Banjo Bill Springs.

Grasshopper Flat – Was originally known as Copple Flat after an early settler who ranged a few head of cattle in the vicinity. When he moved on, the area became a favorite "hunting" ground for fishermen from Jerome who would stop to catch grasshoppers to use as fish bait to catch trout in Oak Creek. It was known as Grasshopper Flat for years until Fanny Mae Gulick found water in the area. Then it became known as West Sedona.

BACON RIND PARK

A number of people have asked where the name Bacon Rind Park came from:

Years ago, when we bought this land, Laura McBride, a granddaughter of Jim Thompson, the original homesteader of this area, told me this story:

In the old days this very land was where people in the area held their Saturday night dances. Refreshed with aged apple or berry juice the people danced all night long to the fiddler. The children would go to sleep on blankets laid on the ground, while the adults enjoyed their dancing and friendships.

During this period a bunch of miners from the mine at Jerome camped on this spot in order to fish in the creek. A storm came up, the creek flooded so much that they were isolated for a few days. In those days you had to cross the creek seven times to get out of the canyon.

They ran out of food and finally all that they had left was the rind from a slab of bacon. This they cut into squares tied a piece of string to each square and you were allowed to chew it for five minutes, then it was pulled from your mouth and someone else got to chew it.

Honestly - the above was the story that she told me.

We had just cleaned out 35 outdated trailers from this area. "Laura", I said, I am planning on building a Park on this area and have been searching for a name for the Park and you have just given it to me - "Bacon Rind Park".

And so today it carries that name "Bacon Rind Park" - Chew on that one for a while.

Bill Garland

Indian Gardens and Bacon Rind Park – I've saved the best for last. Indian Gardens is the area up in Oak Creek Canyon where Jim Thompson, the first settler in the canyon, homesteaded. He found a patch of ground where corn, beans, and squash were growing (the famous "three sisters" of Indian agriculture). It was only natural that the area was then called Indian Gardens. But other old timers referred to the area as Bacon Rind Park. According to the story told to Bill Garland by Laura McBride, a granddaughter of Jim Thompson, how it got that name is a hoot! During that homesteading period (1880s and 1890s) a bunch of miners from Jerome camped on that spot to fish the creek. A storm came up, the creek flooded, and the miners were trapped for several days. Back then you had to cross the creek seven times to get out of the canyon. The miners ran out of food. They had only the rind from a slab of bacon. They cut it into squares and tied a piece of string to each square. Each miner was allowed to chew it for five minutes. It was then pulled from his mouth and someone else got to chew it!

There is a marker at the Park that attests to the story.

FROM HARVEY GIRL TO CATTLE RUSTLER

Let me tell the tragic tale of a Harvey Girl who went astray. Now as you may know, Harvey Girls (who worked in the Fred Harvey Restaurants that provided decent meals along railroad lines in the west) were the epitome of respectability. They were decent, hardworking young women who were provided with room, board, wages and chaperones. The women were said to have helped civilize the American West. Juanita Olive Dove Van Zoast was born in Olivet, South Dakota. The exact date is blurry, but all sources agree that it was sometime between 1892 and 1901. Her mother was Sioux; her father was German, and abusive. After her mother died, the young girl's life became even more grim. At age 14 she ran away from home and made her way through the West. Of necessity, she developed many talents. She also re-named herself Juanita Gale. She was good with horses and with children. She was a capable cook, laundress and housekeeper. In her various travels she connected with the Fred Harvey Company, and managed to talk her way into a job as a Harvey Girl at the newly opened Harvey House at La Posada in Winslow, Arizona.

Juanita had few of the qualifications for the job...she was under age and did not have the required 8th grade education. But she was hired and thought she had died and gone to heaven. The hours were long, but she had fresh clean clothes, a warm bed every night, and regular meals. She had never had it so good!

Like many of the Harvey Girls Juanita met and married a local man and left the Harvey House. Alas, he was already married and was sent off to prison for bigamy. Juanita came back to her job where she met George Creswell, a young man who had a job as a livestock inspector with the Bureau of Indian Affairs. They married, and when she changed her last name to Creswell, she changed her first name to Cecil. Why? Who knows!

The couple had a good marriage until George suddenly died in December of 1936. Cecil struggled financially. As a solution she married again, a man named "Moon" Mullins. Alas, again, Moon was struck by lightning while riding the range in New Mexico. Cecil moved back to Winslow where she tried to make ends meet. She had inherited a homestead from George, and she tried to make the homestead a success. This was during the height of the Depression—no welfare, no social security or any other safety measures.

Cecil was 5'4" and weighed 120 pounds soaking wet. She was forced into a new career: cattle rustler. The locals knew she was doing it, but they also knew she was doing it for food, not for profit. Thus it was a forgiven sin. At one point when she needed a bull to service her cows, she rustled an 800 pound bull, threw him to the ground and dyed him with Red Henna dye. For a full year the owner rode past the bull and didn't recognize him.

The only fly in the ointment was a neighbor, John Thompson, who vehemently argued the property boundary. It escalated into gunfire. No one was hurt but the sheriff was forced to arrest Cecil. When he came to the house, Cecil excused herself, went into another room, locked the door, and shot herself with her .30-30 rifle. She had enough. The locals excoriated John Thompson, and he remained a persona non grata for causing Cecil's suicide. It seems Cecil did not go astray, but was driven astray.

"UNCLE" JIM ROBERTS – GUNSLINGER AND PEACE OFFICER

The days of Bat Masterson and Wyatt Earp were gone. And Jim Roberts, one time top gun in the Pleasant Valley War involving the Grahams and Tewksburys, was semi-retired as the "deputized chief watchman" in Clarkdale, Arizona. "Uncle Jim," as he was known was a true survivor of the Old West...as it really was. His last

Jim Roberts
Photo courtesy Sherman Loy and the Sedona Historical Society

hurrah took place in that unlikely small town of Clarkdale. It was 1928 and he was 70 years old.

Now Uncle Jim didn't fit the mold of the romantic gunfighter or lawman as was portrayed on the pages of the "penny dreadfuls" (dime novels) or on the silent silver screen of the early twentieth century. The kids and adults alike were believing that the make believe heroes were real. Then along came Uncle Jim. Certainly in his prime he could hold his own with the make believe heroes, but when he made his biggest contribution to the legend of Arizona he was looked on as a washed out old geezer. Jim didn't carry a Colt .44 on his hip; his nickel-plated revolver was carried in his hip pocket. He didn't wear a ten-gallon hat or pearl button shirts. He didn't even wear boots, just regular dress shoes like most other folks. Those stories of his past when he joined up with the Tewksburys as one of their deadliest gunslingers, or supposedly single-handedly tamed the town of Jerome (the wickedest community in America) in the 1890s, and had been chief deputy in Cochise County were thought to be tall tales.

On a June morning in 1928, a couple of would be bank robbers drove into Clarkdale with the intent of getting rich. Willard Forrester and Earl Nelson knew that the Clarkdale bank was holding payroll money for the mines. They believed that the old has been cop Uncle Jim would be no problem. On that morning they parked their car in front of the bank, walked into the bank, and, at gunpoint, took $40,000. They locked up the bank employees and customers, walked out with the money and climbed into their car. In the meanwhile, the bank manager managed to get free, grabbed a pistol, ran out into the street and fired the gun. Nelson fired back. Old Uncle Jim, standing by the curb, heard the manager shout that the bank was robbed. He calmly reached into his rear pocket, pulled out his revolver, took deliberate aim with two hands, and fired one shot through the rear window of the car, straight into Forrester's head. One bank robber down. Nelson climbed out of the car, firing a fusillade of shots at Jim while Jim was running toward him. Nelson missed him with every shot! After being tackled, Nelson surrendered.

It was just a day's work for Uncle Jim. He was late getting home for lunch and the food was cold. When his wife told him he should have been home earlier, he just said, "There was a little trouble down town."

The kids in Clarkdale had their real life hero back. Those weren't tall tales, they were real! Jim died in 1934, the last of the Old West peace officers.

V BAR V – THE HERITAGE SITE

You have read about the V Bar V Ranch in its modern metamorphosis, i.e. as homesteads that eventually became part of the University of Arizona. But what about its non-ranching history…its ancient ancestry that reaches back into Paleolithic times? Clues to the ancients who peopled this area centuries ago can be found in the abundance of petroglyphs at this site. Petroglyphs are scratchings/carvings on rock walls as opposed to pictographs which are paintings on rock walls.

Pioneer homesteaders were aware of the "scratching" on the rocks and cave walls, and archaeologists knew about the site since early in the 20th century. But no formal effort to study the anecdotal reports was made until very late in the 20th century (1994). It was through the curiosity of volunteers in Friends of the Forest, especially Ken Zoll, that the solar calendar of the Sinagua people was located and documented on the site. The petroglyphs led to a study of possible ceremonial calendars used to time corn planting and other rituals important to the culture. The site in the Verde Valley was peopled by the Sinagua from ca. 900-1400 A.D. Calendar evidence at the site indicates that this was an agrarian culture. These folks needed to know when the warming and the cooling of the sun as the seasons changed would impact their planting patterns. They created calendars out of rock.

Archaeoastronomy, or cultural astronomy, is defined in "Sinagua Sunwatchers" as the study of the diverse ways in which cultures perceived and integrated objects in the sky into their world view. With nothing but their hands and primitive tools to chip away rock walls these folks were able to create a dependable planting guide…a prehistoric Old Farmers' Almanac.

To date, 1,032 rock petroglyphs have been found at this Southern Sinagua (probably ancestors of the modern Hopi) V Bar B site. Ken Zoll was a docent at the site in 2005 when he noticed the sun coming through two rocks and matching up with concentric circles scratched on another rock. Curious, he took a picture and showed it to an archaeologist who was a bit skeptical. However, he got permission to keep taking pictures. When he showed his film effort to Peter Pilles, there was no argument. A Sinaguan solar calendar was discovered.

The V Bar B Heritage Site is rich with carvings indicating a thriving culture involved in agriculture and trade. Take the time to get a glimpse of days really of yore. Schedule a visit to the site (928-282-3854). And think about what volunteering some of your time to any cause could lead to.

Many thanks to Kenneth Zoll for the information

V BAR V – THE RANCH

When I first heard about V Bar V, it was in conjunction with the petroglyphs located just north of the ranch. The V Bar B was simply the name for this remnant of prehistory. Who knew that a fascinating succession of owners made the history of the ranch itself just as interesting as the ancient site? Dr. David Schafer of the University of Arizona provided the enlightenment.

The land that would become the V Bar V was originally settled by Benjamin Franklin Taylor at the turn of the 20th century. His cattle were branded with the "100" brand and the land became known as the 100 Place. He moved to another area, and in 1915 William Dickinson patented the holding which included 102.5 acres. Two years later it was purchased by two other Dickinsons and David Babbitt. In 1920 those partners sold the ranch (along with another 40 acres) to A.G. Dickinson.

It was not until 1927 that the V Bar V Cattle Company actually came into existence an entity. The 100 Place and a number of small holdings were bought and consolidated by the partnership of Ida May Swift Minotto, Whitey Montgomery, and Omer Maxwell. Ida May was a granddaughter of Gustavus Swift, of the Swift meat packing business...and her husband was a Count. The holding was now known as the V Bar V Ranch, with the right to use that brand. In 1933, the ranch was sold to Marcus J. Lawrence, an eastern playboy who made his mark in the Verde Valley. Lawrence was a womanizer, a boozer, and eventually a homicide victim. The Verde Valley Medical Center in Cottonwood was originally funded by his mother as a memorial to him, the Marcus J. Lawrence Memorial Hospital. When Lawrence was murdered in 1938 by a jealous husband, the ranch became the property of his partner Bruce Brockett.

Brockett entertained many of the movers and shakers in Arizona — including Barry Goldwater — until his death in 1971. The ranch then passed through a number of hands until it was sold to Ben Zink in 1985. In 1995 he traded the original 100 Place headquarters to the U.S. Forest Service and the rest of the V Bar V Ranch and brand to the University of Arizona through a gift/purchase arrangement.

Today the ranch is a model Arizona Agricultural Experiment Station. It runs from Camp Verde 30 miles east, and is between 4 and 5 miles in width. It covers 71,000 acres, 44 of which are private land, and the remainder is Forest Service land. It is a working cattle ranch (550 head), as well as an educational and demonstration facility. Their programs focus on environmental, wildlife and domestic livestock in Arizona and the Southwest. A fascinating place, and to me, even more interesting than petroglyphs.

Many thanks to Dr. David Schafer, Debra Pearson, and the Univ. of Arizona

MAIL IN THE VILLAGE

Most everyone knows that Sedona got to be "Sedona" because Carl Schnebly lobbied for a post office in this area in 1902. Regular mail service for what would become the Village took a little longer.

Before the Sedona post office was established at the Schnebly home near present day Los Abrigados mail was an infrequent service. The mail was dropped off at the train station in Clarkdale about once a week. The post master in Cornville picked it up at the station, took it to Cornville, sorted and delivered it by wagon, going through Cottonwood and Red Rock before arriving at what would become Sedona.

During the years the Schneblys ran the post office, mail was picked up at their home. After they left, the Sedona post office was located in Oak Creek Canyon, near the Thompson place at Indian Gardens. The mail sacks came down from Flagstaff three times a week. When the mail was brought down to Sedona, folks sometimes hitched a ride on the mail wagon to get into town.

Residents of the Big Park area had to go into Sedona for mail service until 1954 when a rural star route service was established. Finally, in October, 1984, a government contract/dispatch station was opened in the Village. Under the direction of Mary Wyatt, who held the contract, the office could sell stamps, money orders, and accept mail, but residents still had to go to Sedona to pick up their mail. According to Mrs. Wyatt, the post office authorities gave her six months to show she could get into the "black" i.e. make money, or they would not renew the contract. Since she had to sign a two-year lease to rent the facility from Andy Hughes there was a lot of incentive to succeed. With the help of businesses that were beginning to locate in the

Village (especially the realtors) she got into the "black" in nine weeks. Once that was accomplished, she could get the boxes that would allow residents to get their mail at the contract station.

The post office facility was located in the building that was built as a ranch home for Fanny Belle Gulick who owned 1000 acres that became the Village of Oakcreek (one word). At one time it was also the office of the Village of Oakcreek Association, named for the Village of Oakcreek.

The post office remained at that location until February, 1997. A much larger building of 6,500 square feet with many "bells and whistles" including a self-service vending machine, a scale and envelopes to prepare mailings opened with a bit of hoop-la. The number of post office boxes tripled to 1,300 to serve a customer base of about 2,650. Tours were given and a special cancellation stamp was available to commemorate the event. The Village mail had arrived.

Thanks to Mary Wyatt and the Sedona Historical Society.

SEDONA'S WALKING ENCYCLOPEDIA

This book has introduced several women who have played a part in the history of Sedona and Red Rock Country. A look into the lives of Sedona Schnebly, Maggie Thompson, Doretta Schuerman, and the colorful Fannie Gulick has provided both knowledge and entertainment. Researching the lives of those admirable women would have been much more difficult had the Sedona Historical Society not been graced with the presence of its own "walking encyclopedia," Edith Smith Denton.

Edith Smith Denton
Photo courtesy Sedona Historical Society

Edith loved history, loved Sedona, and loved the stories of the early pioneers…warts and all. She was a great granddaughter of J.J. (Jim) and Maggie Thompson, the first Anglo settlers in Oak Creek Canyon. The story of her life is a continuing story of growth in the settlement of Sedona.

Edith was born in 1925, just a generation after the initial pioneers found their way into this out-of-the-way corner of Arizona. Her family genealogy includes most of the familiar names from early Sedona. Thompson, James, Purtymun, Smith…they are all part of Edith's heritage. The Thompsons had nine children, one of whom was Lizzie Thompson Purtymun, Edith's maternal grandmother. Her paternal grandparents were Abraham Lincoln and Adda Smith. Their son Roe Nevel Smith married Myrtle Nail (Lizzie's daughter) and bought a 10 acre ranch in Oak Creek Canyon from Frank Thompson, another descendant of J.J. These pioneer families were all intermingled.

Edith lived Sedona's history. She went to Sedona School on Brewer Road, graduating 8th grade in 1939. In 1949 she graduated from what is now Northern Arizona University. She taught school up at Cameron where she had 7 students, both Anglo and Indian, coming to her home for their education. She taught in one room schools at Ash Fork, Crown King, and Punkin Center. She met her husband, Edward Denton, in Punkin Center where she produced a play at the school. She needed a fiddle player for "Ya'll Come," and he came. The Dentons had 3 children. Edith loved history, but she loved fiddle music just as well. She and Edward helped found the Arizona Old-Time Fiddlers Association.

Edith was an active member of the Sedona Historical Society from its beginning. She always said she came by her love of history honestly. After all, her mother, Myrtle Nail

Smith, was the original historical pack rat. Myrtle collected and saved every newspaper, magazine, church bulletin, announcement, etc. that came her way. It provided much of the archival material that was the basis for the original research library of the Historical Society and Heritage Museum. But Edith didn't need the paper work. Ask her any question about Sedona and its history…she could quote you names, dates, relationships, families and feuds from the top of her head. If someone was looking for some obscure little fact of Sedona's history, just "ask Edith." She truly was a walking encyclopedia.

She was officially recognized for her contribution to the preservation of Arizona's history in 2003 when she received the "Al Merito (for merit)" award for non-professional volunteers. Sedona's walking encyclopedia went "out of print" in 2004. The volunteers at the museum still want to "ask Edith."

LET'S HEAR IT FOR THE LADIES

For the most part history has been written about men by men. But how about the women? We must admit it was the civilizing influence of women that really settled the frontier. I've often said I would not have lasted six weeks living under their conditions, so I am in awe of the women who made homes and raised families here in the Arizona Territory. For the next few columns you will be introduced to a few of them. So here's a "huzzah" for some special women who contributed greatly to the settlement of this Red Rock Country and whose names you may not recognize.

MARGARET PARALEE JAMES THOMPSON. Maggie was born in September, 1864, to Abraham and Elizabeth James. She was the sixth of nine children. Her father was a "hard luck" wanderer who moved and removed his family to several locations throughout the west from Arkansas to California, and finally — at the invitation of another wanderer, John James (Jim) Thompson — to the Oak Creek area. Jim and Abraham had become friends while they were both in Nevada. In 1878, when Maggie was 14 years old, the James family spent a year near present Page Springs, and then moved to the Camp Garden area (present day Sedona). Abraham settled down to raise crops and run cattle in this sparsely settled land.

Jim Thompson and the James family remained close. After all, there weren't many people in the area. Jim was past due to settle down and Maggie was approaching marriage age. Was it romance or was it convenience? The barely 16 year old Maggie married 38 year old Jim on October 23, 1880 in Prescott. Maggie had worked hard her whole young life. She was prepared for the tough life here on the frontier. Like her mother, Maggie had nine children. John, the oldest, was born in 1882, and Guy, the youngest, was born in 1911. Think about it. Maggie was pregnant off and on for 30 years. Although the Thompsons did stay in the Oak Creek area, the children were born at various locations: the old Jordan ranch, the Hart ranch, Indian Gardens, and Crescent Moon ranch. Jim had not overcome his wanderlust, and he was gone a lot, but he always came back. Maggie stayed on the land. She tended the kids, the gardens, the cattle and the pigs. She cooked, preserved food, and raised all nine children to adulthood. Jim died in 1917 when the youngest child was six years old. Her grandchildren include Thompsons, Purtymans, and McBrides, familiar names in Sedona history. Maggie died in 1936, honored and respected by her family and her friends.

Next you will meet a very special woman, Dorette Schuerman.

DORETTE SCHUERMAN, A TOUGH LADY

History has shown us that it is often the women who are responsible for the actual settlement of an area, for sinking roots into a new homeland. The women on the western frontier were especially invaluable in bringing civilization this country. They were tough...and they were practical! Such a woman was Dorette Schuerman.

Dorette Scherman
Photo courtesy Sedona Historical Society

You are probably aware of the story of Henry Schuerman, the German emigrant who found his way to Arizona, and who established the hamlet of Red Rock, along Oak Creek. There—one hundred years ahead of time—he would plant the first vineyard and open the first winery in the area, Red Rock Grape Wine.

Dorette Johanna Titgemeyer Schuerman was a practical woman. She was born in Germany in 1855 to a pharmacist and his wife. She was "town people." Dorette's mother died when the girl was only nine. The Schuermans were neighbors who became her second family. Dorette and Henry grew up together. He left Germany when he was 17 to avoid the draft in the Prussian wars. Dorette stayed at home and went to work as a dairy maid. She kept in touch with the Schuermans, and Henry wrote occasionally. When Henry wrote to her in 1884 from Arizona and proposed marriage, Dorette agreed. She was fast approaching 30. She wanted a home and family of her own. She and Henry had a history together. She did not want to die as an old dairy maid. Dorette was a practical woman.

She left Germany and sailed to New York City — not an easy trip--where she and Henry were married. They left for Prescott and eventually for Red Rock Country where Henry had taken title to 160 acres in payment for a debt. Nobody wanted to buy the land located in the midst of a wilderness, so they settled in. Neither was a farmer, they were town people, but they became farmers. They planted orchards and zinfandel grapes that produced a fine wine.

The Schuermans had six children, five of whom lived to adulthood. Clara, their first daughter, died at age 4 from "cholera infantum." Life was not easy. Dorette's first home burned to the ground in 1900, and her second home was flooded by Oak Creek. The Schuermans provided land and material to build the first school in Red Rock. After the school opened in 1891, Dorette provided room and board for the teacher, as well as lodging for the preacher whenever he came through. Her home — and sometimes the school--was a social center in the small settlement. Dorette managed to have a piano hoisted down from Flagstaff to the farm to provide music. When Henry got in trouble with the law for fulfilling his contracts with his winery customers at the start of Arizona's prohibition in 1915--actually getting arrested and spending some time in jail--Dorette did what was necessary to keep the family going.

Henry died in 1920, but Dorette kept active and involved for another twenty years. She got on with life. Dorette died in 1940 at the age of 85. She was one tough, practical frontier woman.

FRANCES WILLARD MUNDS

We have all driven through Munds Park on I-17 when we've headed up the Interstate to Flagstaff. Did you know that in addition to Munds Park there is Munds Canyon, Munds Mountain, and Munds Mountain Wilderness? Who was all this beautiful country named for? Obviously it was a family that left its mark on the Arizona landscape and in Arizona history. And a daughter-in-law, Frances Willard, cemented their place in Arizona history.

Frances Willard Munds
Photo courtesy of Sedona Historical Society

The original Munds to move to Arizona was William Munds, born in Kentucky in 1835. He migrated to Oregon, married, had four children—Jim, John, Neal, and daughter Melvina--moved down the Pacific coast, took a turn to the east, and ended up in Nevada. The wanderlust was still strong, and the Munds family found their way to the Verde Valley. They were cattlemen, and typically their herds wintered in the Valley and summered in the high country.

Jim Munds married Hattie Loy. Jim and his brother-in-law John Loy were responsible for constructing the road that eventually became known as Schnebly Hill Road. John Munds raised horses. Youngest son Neal was, unfortunately, a personification of the adage, "Live fast, die young, and leave a beautiful corpse." Neal was a wild child. When he was 18 (teenagers were not too smart – even back then) he took a dare to ride a nasty tempered outlaw horse. The horse ran into a tree, almost snapping Neal's head off, and then fell on him. Dead at 18. Brother Jim, who had married Hattie Loy, didn't manage to make it to a ripe old age either. In 1891 he was accidentally shot in the head by his own rifle. While herding some horses, he had leaned his gun against a fence; when he returned he carelessly leaned down from his horse to grab the gun. It discharged, striking him in the head. Another young Munds death!

John Munds made up for his brothers' early deaths. He lived to be 83. In 1899 he was elected Yavapai County sheriff. But probably his greatest claim to fame was his marriage to Frances (Fanny) Willard.

Frances Willard Munds was a woman ahead of her time. She was born in 1866, the eighth child of Joel and Mary Grace Willard. She was educated at the Central Institute in Pittsfield, Maine, graduating at age 19. Frances returned to Arizona where she taught school in Pine,

Payson, and Mayer before marrying John in 1890. John and Frances had three children, two girls and one boy. Typical of the age, she stayed home and raised the family, although even then she was active in women's organizations, especially those working for women's suffrage. She was a born politician. She was actively involved in getting the legislature to pass bills granting women the right to vote. These were vetoed by Governor Brodie and later by Governor Kibbey. Frances reached out to the miners union where in a "quid pro quo" the union would support women's suffrage in return for women's support of labor issues.

She was elected chairman of the state suffrage organization. In 1912 Frances helped organize a successful petition drive for a ballot initiative to allow women's suffrage. She then got support of 95% of the state's labor unions. When the Democratic and Republican parties hesitated, Frances threatened to throw the union support to the new Progressive Party. That was pretty convincing. The initiative passed by 3-1 in every county (except Mohave).

Frances went on to be elected state senator in 1915, only the second woman in the country to be elected to the legislature. (You go, girl!) After leaving office, she remained active in politics until she died in 1948. Frances Willard Munds was inducted into the Arizona Women's Hall of Fame in 1982.

SARAH HERRING SORIN - FEMININE TRAILBLAZER

Arizona's past is studded with pioneers of many kinds in many areas. One of the most dynamic trailblazers in the state's history is a woman who ignored the status quo of the Victorian/Edwardian era and lived her life as she wanted, not as society prescribed. She led the way for thousands of her sex...even though she never thought of herself as a feminist or a women's

Sarah Herring Sorin

"libber" (before the terms came into modern usage). Sarah Herring was born in New York City in 1861, the daughter of William Herring, an attorney and eventually a judge. In 1881, Herring moved his family to Arizona where he practiced law in Tombstone, Bisbee, and Tucson. William Herring was Wyatt Earp's attorney of record during the O.K. Corral days.

Sarah was educated to be a teacher, one of the few "respectable" professions for women back then. She spent several years teaching in Tombstone, and actually became a school principal, the first female to hold such a position in that town. Sarah was surrounded by the law; it's what was part of dynamic family discussions. When her brother died in a freak accident, Sarah shifted from teaching to law. William Herring was not a man who believed women belonged in the classroom or kitchen. Sarah admitted that her father was more of a suffragette than she was. Sarah began the study of law under his tutelage in his law office, as was the custom at that time. After a year, she took the equivalent of the Bar Exam, passed with flying colors and was admitted to the practice of law in Arizona. At that time there were fewer than 500 women attorneys in the United States. Sarah then went to New York University, graduating from its law school with honors, finishing 4th in a class of 86 which included 3 women.

In 1896, Sarah and her family moved to Tucson. (Respectable single women continued to live with their families no matter what their age.) In 1898, at the age of 37, she married Tom Sorin, age 52, a noted rancher, newspaperman, and former owner of the Tombstone Epitaph. He was a man not afraid to marry a strong, independent woman. He enjoyed it. Sarah's field of expertise was mining law. She had access to all the players through her husband, but kept their business because she produced favorable court decisions for them. She represented Phelps Dodge, United Globe, and the Old Dominion Copper Company in local, state and federal courts. You can bet the all male juries (no women allowed) were rather flummoxed to see a woman arguing a case before them...and she won most of the time. She won the admiration of both judge and jury.

In 1906, Sarah Sorin was admitted to the Bar of the Supreme Court and was lead defense attorney (first chair) representing Phelps Dodge. In 1912, she was the first woman attorney to argue before the Supreme Court without an accompanying male attorney. She won the case. Sarah Herring Sorin died of influenza in 1914, having blazed a trail for other women. She is in the Arizona Women's Hall of Fame. In 1893, the Arizona Weekly Star wrote what would prove to be a fitting epitaph for Sarah Sorin "...she has asserted her divine right to use the brain, courage, and energy given her. She has thrown the gauntlet to the sterner sex in asserting the right of woman to enter the race of life on equal terms with man."

THE BELLE OF BELL ROCK COUNTRY

Fannie Belle Gulick, one of the more colorful characters in Sedona's recent past, had a major role in the development of both Big Park and West Sedona. She was born in Michigan in 1883. Fanny was married to and divorced from Mr. Gulick long before she came to Red Rock country. Her early history is sketchy at best, but she did get her start to riches in the mining fields of Nevada. She made her first gold strike in about 1907. Fannie used those profits to stake other claims, many of which were successful.

Mrs. Gulick was a shrewd business woman. Diversification was the name of her game. Since prospecting was pretty risky, Fannie moved to Las Vegas and opened a rooming house for miners, a successful operation for more than 40 years. Most accounts agree the rooms were rented on a very short term basis, with accommodating female companions included as part of the room rental.

In the 1940s, she moved to Sedona. Somehow she had acquired about 1000 acres in Big Park and another big parcel in Grasshopper Flats (West Sedona). Fanny had found a new calling. Buying up land became an obsession. The land was cheap because, supposedly, it could not be developed. It was too far from reliable water. Fannie Belle trusted her own instincts—or her own luck—and in 1947 hired Carl Williams, a well driller, who successfully sank a deep well. Fanny got richer.

She always had a soft spot in her heart for her miners. In 1957 she had plans to open "The Fannie B. Gulick Home for Elderly Folks," which would cater to retired miners. The deal never worked out. In 1959 she was offered one million dollars for the Big Park land. She agreed to it if the investors would deliver it to her in cash by March 17, 1959. They had been able to raise $750,000 and would deliver the rest in a few days. Fannie told them to "forget the whole goddam thing" and walked out. (Her language was as colorful as she was, and would make a longshoreman blush.) She later established an "eleemosynary" [charitable] trust which did little but entangle her estate in litigation after her death. Fannie Belle died in 1963 at the age of 80. One of our more colorful locals, Charlie Piper, described her as being "rough as a cob, but a real nice woman." Not a bad epitaph for a lady who lived her life her way.

A RANCH WIFE

The early immigrants to the Red Rock region were characters who came here in the late 19th and early 20th centuries. They found their way here from Ireland, Germany and Missouri. If you skip a generation or so, the next set of immigrants came from places like Connecticut, New York and Minnesota. Their settling into the lifestyle of Red Rock country was a little different, but just as challenging.

Patty Fox with husband and son
Photo courtesy Sedona Historical Society

Patty Fox was born and grew up in Duluth, Minnesota. Her family was definitely upscale. It wasn't until her freshman year in college that she was introduced to the Southwest, and she was hooked on it from day one. Her father had moved to Arizona for health reasons. This was 1947, and Arizona was still pretty rural. She transferred to the University of Arizona to finish college. When her family moved from Phoenix to Cottonwood, Patty happily moved to cattle country with them.

The Red Rock area was pretty sparsely settled in the late 40s and early 50s. In 1935, there were six families in the whole Big Park area. (The 1951 Sedona telephone directory was one page long.) The young adults got to know each other fairly well. Among Patty's new acquaintances was the confirmed bachelor, Kel Fox. Their first meeting was less than romantic, but two years after they met, they married and Patty became a ranch wife.

Ranch life was quite primitive in those days. Because the herd moved from grazing land up in Munds Mountain in the summer to House Mountain in Big Park in the winter, the Foxes had two ranch homes. Their stone ranch house in the Village still stands next to Big Park School. Electric power didn't come into the area until 1949, and that brought running water and, eventually, indoor plumbing. Doing the family laundry was quite a project. Every ten days or so, Patty would take the laundry to the Laundromat in Cottonwood. It had washers, but no dryers. Using canvas, and whatever else she could find to wrap and protect the wet laundry, she would load it in the truck and haul it back to the ranch. The road was dirt, and logging trucks would come roaring over that same road, sending fine red dust through the covering onto the "clean" laundry. When the Foxes got a Kohler generator, Patty got a washing machine with tubs at the ranch. It was outside, so that's where she did the washing…winter and summer.

Both Patty and Kel loved horses, so there was no doubt their boys would grow up on horses. Both Geoff and Grady started riding when they were 3 years old. They all would trail the cattle from summer to winter pastures. The trail up to House Mountain was so steep, the horses would have to be rested six times. Crystal Sky Drive in the Village now crosses that trail.

For years she volunteered at the Cottonwood Hospital, driving from Munds Mountain or Big Park every Friday. In winter Kel, or later one of the boys, would have to plow the drive to the road so she could drive the truck to Cottonwood.

Patty admitted that she loved the ranch life and messing around in a corral. To quote her, she got a kick out of "mucking around in manure." Quite a lady is this ranch wife.

ADMIRAL NELLIE OF THE ARIZONA NAVY

It does seem that most of the interesting, dynamic, charismatic—but unheralded--characters in Arizona's past were women! And one of the best was Nellie Trent Bush. Born in 1888 in Missouri, Nellie and her family migrated to Mesa, AZ in 1893. Nellie knew what it was to work hard for a living. She and her parents lived in a tent, and Nellie worked with her mother to support the family. Her father's health was compromised by a respiratory illness and he was limited in his ability to contribute to the family's well being. Nellie wasn't proud. She washed clothes, worked in the fields, and even in a sugar beet factory.

In spite of these difficulties, Nellie managed to graduate from Tempe Normal School (ASU) with a teaching degree. In 1912 she married a young engineer, Joe Bush. By 1915 Joe, an entrepreneur at heart, moved his pregnant wife to the tiny town of Parker, on the Colorado River, where he bought a river ferry business.

Nellie was no slouch, and she was bursting with energy. She was the first woman to obtain a ferryboat license to navigate the Colorado River, and worked as a pilot for 17 years. In addition, she became a justice of the peace, and in 1920 she was elected to the Arizona State Legislature for a total of 16 years. In 1921 she began law school at the Univ. of Arizona. Nellie had a gift of persuasion. In law school one of the professors banned her (and her fellow classmate, future AZ Supreme Court Chief Justice Lorna Lockwood) from a class discussion on rape. The belief was that this subject was too graphic for women. Nellie went to the dean of the college and asked him if he had ever heard of a case of rape that didn't involve a woman. He had not. Nellie returned to class.

If you have lived in Arizona for any length of time, you know that the biggest issue is WATER. That's a fighting word. When Jimmy Carter wanted to cut back on some government funded water projects, Barry Goldwater warned him, "Mr. President, there's three things a Westerner will fight over — water, women and gold — in that order." Over the years there had been a rivalry between Arizona and California over a number of things, but water was prime. In 1934 it almost caused a shooting war! When a California utility company started building a huge diversion dam on the Colorado River Arizona got ready to draw six shooters. What really ticked the Arizonans was the fact that California was the only state that didn't contribute any water to the river.

The governor called out the AZ National Guard. Nellie loaned them the use of her two small steamboats to reconnoiter the "enemy" shores of California. Unfortunately, these dry land soldiers had never seen a river that had water in it. They got "discombobulated" and got entangled in some steel girders…and had to be rescued by the enemy Californians.

Nevertheless, the media loved the incident. Throughout the country papers wrote about the Arizona Navy and its battleships. Governor Moeur commissioned Nellie Bush as the first and only "Admiral of the Arizona Navy."

Among her many other accomplishments Nellie went on to be admitted to the bar in Arizona and California, to pilot an airplane, to work as a coroner, and was the only woman appointed to the Colorado River Basin States Commission. During WWII she chaired the Women's Division of the Arizona Civilian Defense Council. All this while raising a family! In 1947 she was the only woman appointed to the Colorado River Basin States Commission. Nellie died in 1963, still an active member of the Parker City Council. In 1982 she was elected to the Arizona Women's Hall of Fame.

AN ARIZONA BAD GIRL

Let's have a little fun as I introduce you to a rip-roaring, rootin' tootin' Arizona's BAD GIRL by the name of Pearl Hart, a gal who actually spent some time in the Yuma Territorial Prison. Supposedly Pearl only committed one real crime in her career, but it made her famous throughout the West.

Pearl Taylor

Pearl Taylor was born in Canada in 1876 (or was it 1871? — the records don't agree), to a respectable middle class family. Her father was an engineer who moved the family to Toledo, Ohio when Pearl was two years old. She was well educated. But then, at the age of 17, Pearl fell hard for a bad guy, Frederick Hart. He was a swaggering, seductive gambler who convinced Pearl to elope with him. A disaster in the making!

They made their way to the Columbian Exposition in Chicago where Fred worked as a side show barker, and Pearl was exposed to Wild West shows and strong women like Annie Oakley and Julia Ward Howe. Her life with Fred was indeed a disaster. Not only was he a drunk, a gambler, and unable to hold a job, but he was physically abusive to Pearl. She got the courage to leave him and made her way to Arizona. Her love affair with the West was in full bloom.

Fred found her again, and they got back together for a time — long enough for Pearl to have two children. He hadn't changed, but the lure of the Spanish-American War took him away. Pearl couldn't make it on her own so she wisely sent the children back to her mother in Ohio. Pearl was working as a cook at a mining camp north of Tucson when she met Joe Boot. Some accounts of her life say Pearl was "a cookin' and a hookin'," others say she was a respectable woman trying to get along. She and Joe Boot were working his claim, but had no success finding gold. Pearl then got word that her mother was seriously ill — maybe even dying — and Pearl wanted to see her once more.

Since the claim wasn't producing any gold, she and Joe hatched a plan to rob the stagecoach between Globe and Florence. It was a success. The passengers were robbed, left unharmed, and Joe even gave the passengers one dollar each so they could buy dinner! Alas, the pair's planning was less than good. They got lost, were caught and put into jail awaiting trial. What a sensation! A woman bandit — and one wearing men's clothes, no less. Well, Pearl got cozy with a trustee in the jail. He cut a hole in the wall of her cell and allowed her to escape. But she got caught again.

After their respective trials, Joe was sentenced to 30 years in Yuma Territorial Prison. Pearl got five. She became even more famous in jail. Reporters came to interview No. 1559, and camera men came to take her picture (with a six shooter or rifle, if possible). Pearl was released two years before her sentence expired. She claimed she was pregnant – and only three men had access to her unsupervised…the governor of the Territory, the director of prisons, and the warden. What do you think?

There is no record of Pearl having another child. She just kind of disappeared into the sunset. The most reasonable and well researched account states that she married a rancher named George Bywater and lived quietly near Dripping Springs, AZ until she died in 1955. There are, obviously, some who would dispute this dull end to the famous "Bandit Queen" of the Arizona Territory. I say she deserved the peace and quiet.

A SEDONA LEGEND·

Helen Varner Vanderbilt Frye, sometimes referred to as a Sedona legend, brought glamour to the area when she discovered Red Rock Country in 1941. Twice divorced (her second husband was Cornelius Vanderbilt), she was 33 in 1941when she married Jack Frye, president of TWA Airline. While flying over Sedona, she fell in love with the country. Her love affair with Sedona lasted longer than her relationships with the men in her life.

Helen Varner Vanderbilt Frye
5-29-1974
Photo courtesy Sedona Historical Society

Six months later they bought the old Armijo ranch. They eventually acquired about 700 acres which included parts of the original homesteads of early families. The property became known as Smoke Trail Ranch.

Helen was an exciting personality, and somewhat shocking to the conservative locals. In the language of the day, she was a "hot tomato." She was also an artist with a flair for the unusual. In 1948, the Fryes began construction of another home on the property. She called it the "House of Apache Fires," which sounds romantic and mysterious-- the name came from the campfires of the Yavapai/Apache construction workers camping near the building. There are several stories about the building. One stated that architects from Albuquerque designed the house, but that Elmer Purtymun built it. The home had some intriguing elements: a hanging bed, and a fireplace that could be converted into a water reflecting pool. Unfortunately, the house was never finished. But the marriage was. In 1950 Jack Frye divorced Helen, testifying at the hearing that his business required that he spend his time in the East, and his wife refused to leave Sedona. Helen received four years of alimony and the Sedona property as the divorce settlement. Ironically, Jack Fry, a strong proponent of transportation safety, was killed by a reckless driver in Tucson in 1959.

Helen always followed an esoteric bent in life. She believed in reincarnation, that humans would return after death in the form of an animal. She would never kill any animal, including insects. In 1957 she became involved with Nassan Gobran, the noted sculptor. She never learned not to mix business with pleasure. He planned to buy the House of Apache Fires and turn it into a group home with an art center. He found a backer for the idea, but the backer dropped out when Helen demanded that support for studying flying saucers be part of it. Gobran had to sue Helen to get his down payment back.

Helen continued to be intrigued by the exotic. She became immersed in Eckankar, a philosophical cult. Supposedly she and Gobran were married in an Eckankar ceremony, although there was no legal recognition of the marriage. She continued to sell off property to support herself. Through a Gift Deed from Helen, Eckankar took physical ownership of the acreage that included the House of Apache Fires. Her will, which supposedly was revised to exclude Eckankar, mysteriously disappeared at her death in 1979. Her family sued Eckankar in a probate case that became infamous. The land went through a convoluted series of transfers, but eventually, through the influence of Bruce Babbitt, it became Red Rock State Park. The house sits forlorn and dilapidated, a sad epitaph to a Sedona legend.

RUTH JORDAN – A MIGHTY MITE

The House that Ruth Built – currently known as the Sedona Heritage Museum-- was the home of the Walter Jordan family. Ruth Jordan was the driving force behind the building of the one room cabin that eventually grew to 3000 square feet of modern ranch house. Quite an accomplishment for this tiny mite of a person.

Ruth Jordan
Photo courtesy Sedona Historical Society

Ruth Jordan, nee Woolf, was born in Kentucky in November, 1902. Her family moved to Tempe, Arizona, in 1912. She was a determined young woman. Barely five feet tall, and weighing no more than ninety pounds soaking wet, Ruth had a knack for making things happen her way. Ruth wanted to be a teacher in a rural school. She also wanted a horse (even though she had never ridden a horse). After graduating from Tempe Normal, she got a job teaching at Beaver Creek School. Since she was boarding at Soda Springs Ranch, she had to ride a horse the three miles to the school. She learned to ride quite quickly. At that time women were still expected to wear full skirts when riding. Ruth would have no part of that. Riding astride was tricky enough. Riding side saddle was not to be tolerated. She had a divided leather skirt made and rode it to school, at which time she changed to an "acceptable" skirt.

Ruth had about 20 students ranging in age from kindergarten to 16 years. She herself was quite fastidious and noticed that the youngsters were unkempt. They had head lice and did not wash or groom their hair. Ruth learned that many of them did not have easily available water at their ranches, so how could they wash? She solved that problem (without embarrassing them) by setting one day of the week as "wash day." The girls had their hair washed and curled; the boys had their hair washed and cut. Treatment for lice was applied as needed. Clean hair from then on! When she heard the students were going to play hooky one day, she joined in the fun and said they would all play hooky together. They headed out to Montezuma Castle where they learned about prehistoric Indian ruins while having a picnic.

She met Walter Jordan through his sister, Stella, who had been a fellow classmate at Tempe Normal. It was an instant romance. They made plans to get married, Walter opting for November after the crops were harvested. Ruth said there was no way she was going through a Phoenix summer waiting for a November wedding. Guess who got her way? They were married in July at 5:30 in the morning, while the temperature was still bearable!

In 1931, Ruth and Walter built a one-room cabin on the property he had acquired. At Ruth's behest it was made as comfortable as possible even though it was a single room. There was a sleeping porch, a small shower, an outhouse in the bushes on the north side of the cabin, and a chuck wagon table in the house to allow as much space as possible when meal time was over. Come 1937, Ruth's mother, Fannie Woolf, paid for the addition of two bedrooms and a bathroom with a flush toilet and running water. Of course, Grandma Woolf got to spend the hot summer months in Sedona, not Tempe.

After World War II, Ruth spearheaded the final addition to the house. She oversaw the construction that would double the size of the house. All the modern gadgets, including an electric stove, refrigerator, a bedroom (with a closet!) were all part of the construction. "The House That Ruth Built" was complete.

HELEN HAYDEN: Official Historian of the Village of Oakcreek

Have you ever used the free lending library at the VOCA clubhouse? Did you wonder about the Helen Hayden for whom the library is named? Well, she was something else. She was a petite dynamo who, during her long, active life, outdid the Energizer Bunny. She was a catalyst who helped bring about the realization of VOCA, the Village of Oak Creek Association. And she wrote it all down so the effort would not be forgotten.

Helen Parker Hayden was a New Year's Eve baby, born in 1911. She was one of nine children — a middle child. Helen trained as a nurse and as an x-ray technician. She worked in the medical field for 30 years. Helen was a registered nurse, coordinator and instructor in the School of X-Ray Technology, instructor for medical secretaries and chief technologist of Nuclear Medicine and Radiation Therapy. Most of her career was spent at St. Barnabas Hospital, Minneapolis, where she had been affectionately dubbed "Pee-Wee" [she was 4'10-1/2" tall] by the staff. Her book *Vocabulary Pertaining to Roentgenographic (X-Ray) Reports* has been used to teach nurses and pre-med students throughout the country.

Helen and her husband Frank, who died in 1980, had no children. However, they were world travelers, as Helen continued to be throughout her adult life. She had breathtaking collections to mark her trips to Australia, New Zealand, the South Pacific, China and much of the Far East, and most European countries. She fondly remembered a flight from New York City to London on the Concorde.

How did Helen get here? In 1951, when Helen and Frank Hayden first drove through Sedona on one of their travels, there were no traffic lights, nor was there a West Sedona. In fact, at that time, there were no more than 70 families in the area. But Red Rock country made a lasting impression on the Haydens. They were back in 1962 (Big Park was just a big open park—no Village of Oak Creek), and came back again in the winter of 1967 trailing an Airstream travel trailer. Helen recalls that they stayed in a park in Sedona near the creek. There were two feet of snow that winter, and they had to be winched up to Hwy. 179 before they could get back on their way home. They were sold on this beautiful area. When the Haydens got back to Edina, MN, they put their home up for sale, and within the next year they made the Village their home. Helen was on her way.

HOW OUR VILLAGE GOT TO BE

Hoop-la and whoop de doo. The three years of litigation following the death of colorful Fannie Belle Gulick finally came to an end. In 1967, the Fannie Gulick estate— 920 acres in Big Park—was acquired by Irving A. Jennings, Jr., a Phoenix-based developer, and renamed The Village of Oakcreek. At the same time, according to the developer, he had acquired the Big Park Water Company, which formerly had been operated by Mrs. Gulick. Principals in the firm included Jennings' father, his uncle, and Glenn Snyder, who was chairman of the board of radio station KOY.

There were big plans for the property. Of the 920 acres, 160 were being set aside for recreation purposes, including an 18-hole Robert Trent Jones golf course, along with a skeet range, tennis courts, swimming pools (yes, that is plural), bridle paths, and an upland game club. There were 3,200 residential sites plotted on the remaining 760 acres, with paved roads contoured to fit the rolling terrain. Underground utilities would be installed throughout. Water was not expected to be a problem...Jennings' experts had advised him that there was plenty of water in Big Park at about 600 feet, and there would be no difficulty in providing water for residences, the golf course, swimming pools, and other facilities planned.

Now came time for the Big Sell. On Memorial Day weekend, 1967, the Village of Oakcreek held its official ground-breaking ceremonies. The celebration lasted four days. The then Governor Jack Williams and Congressman Sam Steiger headed a delegation of political luminaries who took part in the opening ceremonies. There were quarter horse races with minimum purses of $200. The chief pilot for Mesa Flight Service would perform high speed loops and rolls in a P-51, and a 19 year old professional aerobatic pilot was scheduled to demonstrate inverted flying, snap rolls and Cuban 8s while flying a Champion Citabrias. All this to sell year round vacation and retirement homes.

By November of 1967, the developer had sold a little over 30 homesites. The first home built in the development belonged to Mr. and Mrs. W.E. Lamb, Jr., of Tucson. Progress was slow, but fairly steady. The first nine holes of the golf course were opened in September, 1969, with a head to head match play game between Miller Barber and Bob Rosburg. They played the nine hole course twice, with Barber winning $5000 and Rosburg $3000. They each also received a Village of Oakcreek homesite. A December, 1969, ad in the *Verde Independent* indicated that 700 homesites had been sold, and that plans were under way to develop a 5 acre lake and a grassy amphitheatre for open-air entertainment. It also stated that the Dooleyville riding stables were up and running. (Where are they now, you ask?) Dooleyville was to be the name of an "old-new" western town in Big Park. When plans for the town were aborted, the stables disappeared.

In late 1971 there were 62 actual residents in the Village of Oakcreek. On May 27, 1972, the second nine holes of the golf course opened without nearly as much hoop-la as with the first nine. A new shuttle service, with a double-decker English touring bus, running between the Village of Oakcreek, Sedona, and Slide Rock, carried signs advertising Oakcreek homesites and an audio system lauding life in the Village of Oakcreek. Does this sound familiar? Like Sedona time share sales today?

All was not well with the developers. 1972 was not a good year for them. The LOL (Lot Owners League) was created to thwart a number of questionable, heavy-handed pronouncements from the developers, a.k.a. Big Park

Development Company and the Village of Oakcreek Association. The games were on!

Many thanks to the Sedona Historical Society and to Helen Hayden's Village of Oakcreek History.

VILLAGE OF OAKCREEK – AN ONGOING SAGA

The Village of Oakcreek had its beginning in 1967 when Fannie Gulick's 920 acres in Big Park were acquired by developer Irving Jennings. There were 3,200 residential sites plotted, but only 30 were sold in the next six months. By 1970 (after offering free green stamps and other incentives) 700 homesites had been sold. In 1971 the State of Arizona Real Estate Board ordered a "halt sales" because the Developer (Big Park Development Company) had failed to provide promised amenities. The Developer then tried to coerce property owners to channel all sales or resales through its own company, excluding local realtors. This was not only unenforceable, but also illegal.

The Developer then incorporated the newly formed Village of Oakcreek Association with the same officers as the parent company. A notice was sent to each VOC property owner demanding payment of assessments, including retroactive monthly charges, for a total of 18 months. The property owners were incensed. A protest meeting was held in December 1971, and by January 1972 the Lot Owners League (LOL) was formed and authorized as an Arizona corporation. Its mission was to tame the chicanery and apparent mis-management of the Developer. By August of that year Jennings, a Developer Principal, found himself in trouble legally with HUD and other government agencies because of development deals in New Mexico and California. He was accused of failure to provide clear titles, improper use of assessment funds, failure to hold proper elections, and outright fraud.

Enter Ray Hose. He was "the right man in the right place at the right time" according to Village folks who lived through hullabaloo. His background included an engineering degree, various CEO positions, and partnership in an oil refining business. He knew government and legislatures. Ray took on the challenge of ordering the chaos that was known as the Village of Oakcreek.

The original committee that formed the LOL included Ray Hose and Helen Hayden. Ray researched the Developer's charter and learned it had not complied with its own directives. It could also change the by-laws at will. Ray found a hidden legal notice announcing a board meeting of the Developer set at "ten minutes before two." Twenty-five LOL members showed up at the meeting site which was set with four chairs. The LOL sued for non-performance. Hose wrote letters to every lot owner informing each of the situation. Ray put up a $20,000 line of credit to back the lot owners in their legal battle. An existing Arizona statute which provided that taxes could be prorated to sold lots from those that had not been sold was challenged and changed. Two slates were set up for the board election, one for the Developers and one for the Villagers. He arranged for the election to be held at the Elks Club—no mail-in vote. The Villagers won seven to one. Thanks, Ray.

VILLAGE OF OAKCREEK – FINALLY

From 1974 through 1980, the organization that would eventually become VOCA (the Village of Oak Creek Association) went through some agonizing growing pains. In January 1975, APS turned off the power for the wells that watered the golf course. A $2500 cash deposit was made to APS to continue service, which was certainly cheaper than having to replace greens and fairways. The Developer (Big Park Development Company) closed its sales office and dismissed all its employees. It was looking for a buyer for its marketable asset, the golf course. The Developer was in a world of hurt. What goes around comes around, and all its fraudulent machinations in the previous years had come back to hurt it. The Developer had reneged on loans, on taxes, on promised facilities (water, streets, sewers, etc.) and had employed deceptive sales practices. Deliveries for fertilizer and weed control chemicals for the golf course were made on a C.O.D. basis. The Developer had long neglected the course and revenue failed to meet expenses, causing a real cash flow problem. Property owners were solicited for funds and notes in $1000 units were issued.

The golf course was acquired by the Village of Oakcreek Association under the control of the property owners. VOCA then assumed the mortgage indebtedness and cleared other encumbrances leading to a total cost of $400,000 for the acquisition of the golf course. In 1977 the golf course trails were resurfaced for a cash amount of about $1000 plus a lot of "sweat equity" of the Men's Golf Club members as they distributed 250 tons of material.

The financial problems that had to be surmounted were enough to turn any CPA to drink, but they were successfully overcome, even though it took years. An ambulance service was established in 1978. Construction of the Wild Turkey Townhouses was begun. When the Big Park Water Company informed the VOCA Board that it could not supply water for summer irrigation of the golf course, VOCA drilled a new well on its property. The post office established Rural Route #3 — this meant that mailboxes were moved to individual residences, no longer long racks at the highway entrances. VOCA employees were covered by health insurance. Golf club membership initiation fees were set at $500.

By 1980 plans for the original Community Center were well under way. Rest room facilities had been built on both nines. VOCA owned four wells, three of them on the golf course. The Circle K provided convenience shopping; Plaza del Sol functioned as a shopping center; and the VOCA office moved from Jordan Road in Sedona to Fanny Gulick's old ranch home (Ranch House Square along S.R.179) in the Village. Most important, nine years after the property owners united to form the Lot Owners League and six years after they took responsibility for the management of VOCA (with a bank balance of $721.18 and no assets), VOCA's credit rating was excellent, with bills being promptly paid. Those "village people" had done it!

VILLAGE OR PARK, WHICH IS IT?

Several years ago the Sedona Red Rock News ran an informal and "irreverent" survey of locals to determine if anyone understood the difference between the Village of Oak Creek and Big Park. The results were interesting and amusing. So let's have a little retrospective.

What is essentially known as the Village is part of the 1000 acre estate of Fanny Belle Gulick, one of the most colorful residents of Red Rock Country. After her death in 1963, much of the property was acquired by Irving Jennings, a Phoenix-based developer, who intended to turn the sparsely settled area into a "masterplanned 920 acre residential-recreational resort community in the Oakcreek-Red Rock country." He named it "The Village of Oakcreek" (one word). Why? Only he knew. The rest of the story of the problems, struggles, machinations, etc. of the development has been addressed in earlier columns, and especially in Helen Hayden's book "Village of Oakcreek History: A Concatenation of Events."

Big Park, like all "parks" here in the West, is basically a large, relatively flat piece of land surrounded by buttes and mesas, i.e House Mountain, Courthouse Butte, Lee Mountain, and Horse Mesa. Dry land farming and ranching were the methods of scratching out a living. At the turn of the century, a few small, ultimately unsuccessful homesteaders staked claims here. From the 1930s on Kel Fox operated a cattle ranch that eventually was a success. But that was the exception, not the rule. It was pretty much open, empty land.

Big Park is an informal designation, not named on official Forest Service maps, although the Village of Oakcreek is. So it is no wonder the folks surveyed by the Red Rock News were confused. One woman responded that she had never heard of Big Park, but that the Village of Oakcreek worked for her. Another questioned if there was a difference, or did they mean the same thing? A teenager thought the school was named Big Park, but that the Village was where everybody lives. One erudite gentleman stated that there was no difference, except some "bozo bananahead" decided to call it Big Park. Joanne Johnson had the clearest answer. Big Park is the entire expanse of flat land, but the Village includes the community's commercial area and nearby residential areas. The whole community is unincorporated Yavapai County and no lines of demarcation have been established. For years, however, the highway department signs as you enter from either direction identify the "Village of Oak Creek" (two words). Very interesting!

So what do you think? Is it the Village, a Park, or does it really matter? It is just part of the wonderful confusion of place names endemic here in Red Rock Country.

WHAT'S IN A NAME?

A rose by any name would smell as sweet. A rock by any name would still be the same rock. But the same rock, indeed, can bear more than one name, at least here in greater Sedona.

Abraham James — one of the original settlers — is often given credit for naming many of the rock formations. Steamboat Rock, Table Mountain (also known as Table Top Mountain), Bell Rock and House Mountain were named by him in the 1870s and 1880s. There is some question, though, as to whether he or Maggie Dumas named House Mountain.

One of the classic controversies is present day Cathedral Rock near Red Rock Crossing. According to the reminiscences of the old-timers, that sandstone peak near the crossing was called Court House Rock. The maps of the general land office did show the name to be Court House Butte. It was sometimes referred to as Castle Rock, according locals. What was known as Church House Rock or Cathedral Rock is the butte east of Bell Rock in Big Park. A cathedral is much more impressive than a church, so that name became more popular, certainly in recent years. According to legend, the first Forest Ranger stationed in Sedona got the two rock names mixed up on his maps, and that is the reason Court House Rock is at the north end of Big Park and Cathedral Rock stands watching over Oak Creek Crossing.

Did you ever wonder what Snoopy Rock was called before Charles Schulz drew the comic strip in 1950? According to Charlie Piper, an old time local, it had no name. It was merely the southwest end of a rock called Camel Head Rock. Once you became familiar with Charlie Brown and Snoopy, it didn't take too much imagination to see Snoopy on his back on top of his dog house. Sometimes that southwest end was referred to as the Sphinx. Are you thoroughly confused now?

Little Horse Park, which includes the Chapel area, was once owned and farmed by the Pipers. It was a big open space with a magnificent rock escarpment to the north. Two pinnacles guarded the rock formation which stood on

Little Horse Park

Forest Service Land. They were known as the Twin Peaks. When Marguerite Staude, with the help of Barry Goldwater, brought the Chapel of the Holy Cross into being, the Twin Peaks evolved into the Nuns. It does seem appropriate to have two big, tall nuns protecting the chapel. Now there were also some other names given to certain rock structures in the area, names given by adolescent boys in the 30s and 40s. However, they cannot be printed in a family newspaper. They are hilarious, but not G-rated, not even PG.. If you run into some of the old-timers, ask them. They just might tell you.

This article would not be possible without the wonderful archival material at the Sedona Historical Society and the memories of guys like Charlie Piper.

RED ROCK VORTEXES

In the past thirty years the "vortexes" of Sedona have become almost as famous as the Red Rocks. Tourists by the thousands make their pilgrimages to be energized, to meditate, or to have their curiosity satisfied. Sedona has been called the (unofficial) New Age capital of the world. According to a study done by Northern Arizona University 64% of the near 4 million visitors who come to Sedona come for a spiritual experience! (There are many psychics who make their homes here.) Sedona is second only to the Grand Canyon as a tourist attraction. And whom do we have to thank for this influx of tourist dollars? A psychic named Page Bryant.

Around 1980, Page Bryant, now living and writing in North Carolina, was temporarily living in Sedona. She psychically channeled an "entity" who described several different energy spots here in Red Rock Country. Ms. Bryant named them "vortexes." Jeff Ngilski, a local hair stylist who lived here 35+ years, recalled Bryant sitting in a chair in his salon with a map of Sedona spread out before her, geographically locating the vortexes. He suggested that Airport Mesa would be good since it was easily accessible to people. It was, and it caused problems on the landing strip. The vortex cooperatively moved about a half mile down Airport Road to the saddle where it is now located. Ms Bryant's audio tape about vortexes and earth energy (found in the Sedona Public Library) mentions only the current site of the Airport Vortex.

According to Ms. Bryant vortexes are either electrical (positive), magnetic (negative), or electro-magnetic (balance of both). The electric exhibit a male force and charge or vitalize the physical body. The magnetic exhibit a female force and are receptive to the psychic subconscious mind.

There are seven vortexes in Red Rock Country. Only four are usually discussed. The largest is Boynton Canyon. It is electro-magnetic with a powerful energy that promotes physical and emotional healing. It is located off Dry Creek Road in West Sedona in the general area west of the Seven Canyons development. According to Ms Bryant the Yavapai consider that to be sacred land and the area may be under the protection of the "grandfather spirits" who make it difficult to develop sacred land.

Cathedral Rock is an astral, magnetic vortex promoting past life recall, among other phenomena. The above mentioned Airport Vortex is electrical. It stimulates the consciousness and alleviates depression. Bell Rock is the most interesting vortex. It is electrical and powerful. It not only resembles a bell, but it also resembles the Gemini space capsule (again, according to Ms Bryant). Energy emanates from the center of the rock to the heavens; it is a beacon. At least all the folks who gathered for the Harmonic Convergence in 1987 thought so.

The other three vortexes are not nearly so romantic. The Hyatt Hotel/Post Office is a very small vortex centered on the hill which includes the Chamber of Commerce Building. Supposedly, it is more like a time warp that causes temporary confusion, disorientation, and foul-ups. Not really good vibes for a post office, retail shops and a hotel. Indian Gardens is a unique, man-made vortex. It doesn't do much. It is temporary and will dissipate in time. Ms. Bryant said she learned of this vortex through psychic reception. Apache Leap is located across 179 from Bell Rock. It is very negative. She received psychic knowledge (which she admits she was unable to verify) of a group of Apaches being chased up the cliffs by the cavalry. The Apaches chose to leap from the cliffs rather than be taken prisoners. Did anyone ever attempt to ride a horse up the face of that hill?

Articles have been written debunking the whole vortex idea. Some say Sedona is a town built on a hoax, while others believe it is a holy place. And while most of us who live here take the notion of magical vortexes with a big grain of salt, we did find our way here from somewhere else. Now that is your woo-woo thought for the day.

Photo of Airport Vortex

THE HARMONIC CONVERGENCE – A REMEMBRANCE

Whoa, folks, do you realize that August 16 and 17 marks the anniversary (1987) of the Harmonic Convergence right here in our Village of Oak Creek? A quarter of a century. Time sure does pass when you're having fun!

For those of you not conversant with New Age/New Wave, or were not living here twenty years ago, let me entertain you. It is the moment outlined in ancient Mayan calendars to note "the precise calibration points in a harmonic scale that marks the moment when the process of global civilization climaxes." It was the"dawning of the Age of Aquarius"—shades of "The Fifth Dimension" with harmony and understanding. There are twelve "power points" or sacred sites worldwide, and Sedona is one of them. It has some pretty august company: Stonehenge, Mt. Olympus, the Great Pyramid, Machu Picchu, and Mt. Fuji, plus a few others not quite so notable. Not only did the Mayan calendar mark the date, but astrologically, the planets cooperated. A Grand Triune, the alignment of seven planets, occurred between August 14-20, 1987.

Local believers took the event very seriously. Organizers of the "world harmony days" anticipated thousands of celebrants to extol the evolutionary shift from separation and fear to unity and love. Celebrations were expected from international to local levels. In Sedona a free newsletter was available, along with a "hot line" to keep devotees informed as to exact times and places for the various events. The key event was seven minutes of humming at noon Greenwich time (5:00 a.m. Sedona time) by those seeking to usher in the era of peace and harmony. (Just try humming for seven minutes.)

Bell Rock

Rumors abounded. A space ship would be landing on Bell Rock...Bell Rock would crack in two and the Mother Ship would fly from Inner Earth to Outer Space...the Sunday morning humming was to levitate Bell Rock since Bell Rock was to be the spaceship. Devotees were dancing naked around Bell Rock—wishful thinking? The most dreadful rumor was that there would be a human sacrifice off Apache Leap (west of Bell Rock).

Traffic along Hwy. 179 was pretty horrendous, much like holiday weekends today. Cars were parked from the Circle K northward to the "roller coaster." Remember, this was before SR179 was reconfigured. Flashlights lit the north face of Bell Rock like giant fireflies. Lights from airplanes illuminated the sky over the big red butte. A trio of Bible students said they saw the stars turn green and a group of stars around the moon change into the shape of a cross—a sign out of Revelation. The Forest Service counted 1,800 folks on Bell Rock, and motels logged in over 4,000 reservations in town. Three Phoenix television stations were shooting the activity at Bell Rock.

The event certainly helped business to boom. Crystals were for sale on every street corner. Coffee Pot Restaurant (just about the only available eating place in town) was packed from before opening to after closing. What a time! Of course, some detractors nick-named the event the "Moronic Convergence," and one local pundit quoted Captain James Kirk, "Beam me up, Scotty. There's no intelligent life down here." Was there no romance in his soul? Lest you think this is a product of my imagination, all this information was gleaned from newspaper accounts of the day, both the Arizona Republic and the Sedona Red Rock News.

Archived records courtesy Sedona Historical Society

WINERIES IN RED ROCK COUNTRY

Have you noticed the proliferation of wineries here in Red Rock Country? There are at least six commercial wineries and an uncounted number of private or "hobby" wineries. While it seems like a new and unusual industry for Arizona, it's actually a rebirth of an industry begun by an early pioneer of this country, Heinrich Schuerman.

Heinrich was born in Melle, Germany in 1852. He left there when he was seventeen years old, avoiding conscription into the Kaiser's army to fight in the constant wars plaguing Europe at that time. He made his way to Canada and then to the United States. For the next ten years he worked his way through this country, eventually heading west, ending up in Prescott, Arizona.

In Prescott, Heinrich (now Henry) and a cousin ran the old Pioneer Hotel from about 1880 until 1885. In 1882, he had taken deed to farmland on Oak Creek in payment of a $500 personal debt owed by Tom Carrol, who earlier had homesteaded land in what is now West Sedona. In 1884, Schuerman traveled to New York to marry his childhood friend, Dorette Titgemeyer, who had emigrated from Melle. In 1885, Henry and Dorette traveled to Red Rock Country to look at the land, fully intending to sell it. After five days of travel from Prescott to Big Park, and finally across Oak Creek, they reached what would become the settlement of Red Rock (near Red Rock Crossing). They had no intention of staying, but they could not give the land away, much less sell it. It was too remote. The land was too good to abandon. They didn't know what else to do so they settled in. Henry had a plan. They were not farmers, but they planted crops, including an orchard and a vineyard. With a vineyard, it became expedient to build a winery. They may have been too far from large markets for fresh produce, but they were less than twenty miles from Jerome, approaching its heyday at the time. It had a growing population that eventually reached near 15,000, 12,000 of whom were thirsty copper miners. They were equidistant from Fort Verde, and the military have been known to indulge in the juice of the grape. Red Rock Grape Wine was born and was thriving. The Schuermans enjoyed prosperity.

Unfortunately, during the successful period, Henry found out that Thomas Carrol did not have legal title to the land! Henry had to repurchase the land from the railroad company that actually owned it. The winery continued to be successful, allowing Henry a comfortable lifestyle.

All went well until 1915 when Arizona passed a prohibition law five years before the federal law. Henry's trade made him a lawbreaker. He spent some time in jail for illegal winemaking, later being pardoned. Henry died in 1920, the first winemaker in Red Rock Country. Wouldn't he be amazed at all those following his footsteps today?

Early photo of Schuerman
Winery
Courtesy of Sedona Historical Society

HOLIDAYS AMONG THE RED ROCKS

How did the old-timers ever manage to celebrate the holidays before shopping malls, WalMart, and Toys "R" Us catalogues mailed out before Labor Day? They certainly didn't worry about crowded airports, highway traffic jams, or getting gifts mailed out of state by the first week in December. No, the old-timers had parties, usually on Christmas Eve, where everyone within walking or riding distance could come together to have a good time.

The get togethers were held at one of the local one-room schoolhouses, the only place big enough to house a dance--which was a necessary part of any pioneer party. Families came together, from the grandparents to the babes in arms. Everybody came. If the youngsters weren't old enough to dance, they would nap on chairs pushed against the walls. Everyone else danced to the music provided by the fiddlers. Good fiddlers were as sought after as current rock stars. The most popular dances included the one-step, the two-step, waltzes, and "put-your-little-foot." Many of us of a certain age remember the last one, even today. Just hum it to yourself. Two other dances added to the boisterous entertainment. The "broom dance" was a great mixer. Everyone on the floor had a partner except one person with a broom. When the broom was dropped with a crash, everyone changed partners. "Scrounge about" was quite a cozy dance. It was so named because the floor was so crowded the couples had to dance really, really close together for all to fit. That was called "scrounging" together.

Of course, there were always refreshments. Folks brought cakes and pies. And for those who cared to imbibe, there was always "Uncle's Hooch," sometimes called white mule...white lightning...corn squeezin's, or booze (called that because early whiskey bottles were marked with the bottlemaker's name, Booze).

Christmas trees were usually blue spruce or pinon, cut down in Oak Creek Canyon. They were decorated with chains of colored paper and strings of popcorn—no twinkling tree lights; electricity didn't come to the Red Rock area until decades later. A home made star often topped the tree.

At midnight, a five gallon can was set on a campfire outdoors to make coffee, boiled cowboy style, and the pies and cakes were brought out. Everyone feasted. It wasn't unusual to go back to dancing until dawn. And a good time was had by all.

Come New Year's the celebrating would continue. The late Laura Purtyman McBride recalled how her father, Albert Purtyman, would slip away in the early morning after the family was asleep, head up into Oak Creek Canyon, and set off dynamite charges blasting high in the rocks. According to Mrs. McBride, it woke everyone to the new year.

The old-timers certainly had a more laid back approach to the holidays. Jennie Lee Van Deren shared her recipe for a Holiday Custard Cup that called for 12 cups of milk, 12 tablespoons of sugar, 12 eggs, ½ teaspoon of salt. Separate eggs, beat egg yolks with sugar, add to milk, and cook slowly, stirring constantly, until it thickens and coats the back of a spoon. THIS WILL TAKE 1-1/2 TO 3 HOURS, SO DRAW UP A TALL STOOL AND A GOOD BOOK. Beat egg whites until stiff, beat custard into egg whites slowly. Add vanilla, cinnamon, and nutmeg to taste. Cool completely. Add 12 ounces of bourbon, rum or brandy just before serving.

It was the highlight of the holiday meal. I can understand why it was created only once a year, on a very special occasion.

YAVAPAI APACHE NATION – OUR NEIGHBORS TO THE SOUTH

When we think about the Yavapai-Apache Nation (YAN) to the south of us, we think of Cliff Castle Casino with its gambling tables and great restaurants. But it is the story of the YAN that is worth hearing.

The YAN were at one time two distinct tribes: the Yuman speaking Pai and the Athabascan speaking Apache. They co-existed in the Verde Valley for centuries, moving seasonally as they followed the deer, agave, corn, melons, etc. Their relatively peaceful existence came to a halt with the discovery of gold in the Prescott area in 1863. It was the beginning of the end. When the Civil War ended, the federal government and the military were free to conquer the American West...and they did so with vengeance. The period from 1863 to the turn of the century was, in effect, the Native American version of the Holocaust.

In 1871, President Ulysses Grant established military reserves to hold the Indian populations. The Rio Verde Reserve was created along the Verde River – 800 square miles northwest from Camp Verde. From 1871 to 1873 the Yavapai and the Apache on the Reserve were subjected to systematic reduction through bad water, inadequate rations, and the slaughter of their holy men and leaders. They were simply taken out and shot. In the winter of 1875, under an executive order of the president, 1500 Yavapai and Apache from the Rio Verde Reserve were marched 180 miles to the San Carlos Reservation. Hundreds of lives were lost along with thousands of acres of treaty lands promised to the people by the federal government. Indian Commissioner Dudley did not allow use of wagon roads that could be used to transport supplies as well as the sick and elderly. Dudley made them all—young and old—walk through mountain passes and narrow canyon trails in the mid of winter to get to San Carlos. Half the population died. The Yavapai Apache commemorate that day as "Exodus Day."

Apache woman, 1880

By 1900 the military reservation system had become defunct. People simply walked away. Only about 200 actually made it back to their homeland. Their land had been taken over by white settlers. Between 1900-1934, the people re-acquired 640 acres in the Verde Valley. The Indian Reorganization Act of 1934 morphed the two tribes into the Yavapai Apache Nation.

The Eisenhower administration terminated all reservations. Congress passed laws allowing Indians to sue for lands usurped during the westward expansion. In 1956 the Yavapai and Apache together filed a lawsuit for 10,000,000 acres of homeland, which they eventually won at the 1873 value of fifty cents per acre. After legal' fees and distribution to the tribes, the Camp Verde nation received $3,000,000.

The change of pace over the past 125 years has been phenomenal. The YAN has established the Casino, a gravel company, a cement plant, and an RV park, while focusing on the renewal of traditional skills, crafts, and ceremonials. A daunting task.

Research material and photo courtesy Yavapai Apache Nation

PUSHMATAHA---WHAT?

I thought it might be fun to digress just a bit and still look at "days of yore," but focus on a name. Almost everyone in this area has attended — at least once-- a function at the Pushmataha Center located on Brewer Road. How did it get that name? Who or what was "Pushmataha?" William Howard, scion of one of the original pioneer families, wrote in 1982 that the structure on Brewer Road was originally an antiques gallery, then became an artists' studio. It found its way into private ownership and eventually became the property of Keep Sedona Beautiful. According to Howard, the name "Pushmataha" in big bold letters was always on the building. Unfortunately, the "how" and the "why" of the name seems to have been lost, but not the "who."

Pushmataha was a Choctaw Indian born in Mississippi in 1764. The Choctaws were one of the "Five Civilized Tribes" which included the Cherokees, the Chickasaws, the Creeks, and the Seminoles. They acquired that name because they codified their laws, developed a written language, established schools, and printed books in their native language. The Choctaws in 1834 produced the first written constitution adopted within the present state of Oklahoma. They were hardly ignorant savages.

While still in his teens, Pushmataha distinguished himself in warfare. As the years went by he continued to add to his reputation. He became a chief, and then a mingo (a kind of super-chief). It was through his efforts that friendly relations were established and promoted with the Whites. When the great Shawnee chief Tecumseh met with the Choctaw to persuade them to join with him and the English to fight the Americans during the War of 1812, it was Pushmataha who opposed the movement and sided with the Americans. Tecumseh's mission failed.

Pushmataha was highly respected by the American military. He fought both the English and the Creeks who had allied with them. While aiding the American troops, he was so tough in his discipline that his wild warriors were converted into efficient soldiers. His energy and success in fighting the Creeks and the Seminoles earned him the nickname "The Indian General." He negotiated and signed many treaties. In one treaty, he demanded that 54 sections of eastern Choctaw land—land they would give up—be surveyed and sold at auction, and the monies collected would go into a special fund for education of Choctaw youth in their new land in Oklahoma.

Pushmataha died in 1824 in Washington, D.C. while negotiating another treaty. He was 60 years old. He was buried with full military honors in the Congressional Cemetery, with a funeral cortege of 2000 people, including President Andrew Jackson. His eulogy was pronounced in the U.S. Senate by John Randolph of Virginia.

A county in Oklahoma bears his name, as does a Boy Scout Council in Mississippi. His portrait hangs in the Mississippi Hall of Fame, and his name boldly identifies the Keep Sedona Beautiful building in Arizona. Maybe it's not important to know "why" or "how ."

THE ROAD. . .THE ROAD

The Village and the City came together in a joint effort to keep the charm and beauty of Red Rock Country intact in spite of the State trying to shove "progress" down our throats. This is a history of days of yore not so long ago.

The first road accessed by homesteaders through Big Park was a dirt road that wound its way through Grasshopper Flat (now West Sedona) through Red Rock (the old Henry Schuerman homestead) across Oak Creek to Little Park (now Verde Valley School Road), then south on what eventually became SR179. This road, like the road through Oak Creek Canyon and Schnebly Hill Road, was the result of efforts by the citizens who lived along the way. Grass roots toil and travail succeeded when government was not involved.

Old State Route 179
Photo courtesy Sedona Historical Society

It wasn't until after 1900 that a dirt road was created to connect Big Park with the hamlet of Sedona. (Remember, T.C. Schnebly didn't get the federal o.k. to name the post office Sedona until 1904.) Over the decades the road was improved with gravel, but it was not until 1948 that actual paving was begun. It was done in three sections finally completed in December 1961. There was a big official celebration to open "Access Road 179" from Sedona to the Black Canyon Highway. However, I-17 was not officially completed as an Interstate until 1976.

By 1987, SR179 was a well established connector between I-17 through the Village of Oak Creek to the town of Sedona. And, in fact, it had been designated by the state as the "Red Rock Scenic Road." It became heavily used by tourists who were intrigued by the mystical enticement of Sedona. It was also in need of repair and maintenance.

In 1992, ADOT (Arizona Department of Transportation) looked at the situation and decided that a divided 4-5 lane highway from I-17 to Sedona was the answer. Whoa! Cooler heads among the citizenry of the Village and of Sedona protested, and in 2000 the Sedona City Council made an official protest to the state regarding ADOT's decision. Another chance for a grass roots effort to get done what the people wanted, not what the bureaucrats wanted. The landscape between the Village and Sedona is strikingly beautiful. Did it make sense to rush traffic through it at highway speeds? The local media supported ADOT's plan, but the people did not. They spoke out, they organized, and "Voice of Choice" was born. Beginning in 2000, twenty-seven men and women served on its board of directors, attending weekly meetings for four years. It was a motley crew that gave of its time, talent—and treasure. Voice of Choice. reached out to the general population for moral and financial support, and it worked.

Expert professionals were hired who disputed ADOT's findings. V.O.C. reached up all the way to the governor, and found support from Janet Napolitano (it helps when it's an election year). ADOT backed down and began to work with the people. The process that was instituted included "charrettes," information sessions that all concerned citizens could understand. And those concerned citizens were legion. Options for the road were presented and voted upon. We are currently driving on the winning option.

State Route 179 as completed in 2014
Photo courtesy D. Benore

At the beginning of the process one of the Voice of Choice board members, David Benore, researched and presented a "white paper" on round-abouts to ADOT, hoping one or two would be built in the Village. ADOT and the people fell in love with round-abouts! You see the result. Another committee formed to work on getting the road named an "All American Road," which would open the door for grants to finance "goodies" (median landscaping, street lights, benches, trash containers) not covered in the road building. The grass roots movement kept on going. An adjunct committee initiated a special Special Improvement District to fund a continuing maintenance district—an agreement to tax themselves—and it succeeded. Citizens in control!

ADOT did all right, too. It won an international award for the process that was born right here. And everyone was a happy camper.

ARIZONA – NEVER DULL

Continuing the 100th birthday year of Arizona, the following piece could be entitled "tidbits of trivia" or "oodles of oddities." Now, geographically speaking, only 15-17% of the total land area is privately owned, 28% is Native American land, and the rest is public land, forests, parklands, and recreation areas. Were you aware that Arizona encompasses 113,998 square miles, while the United Kingdom has only 93,784 square miles, and the state of Massachusetts has all of 10,555 square miles? Back in 1863 when Arizona officially became a United States Territory, there were four "humongous" counties: Yavapai, Yuma, Pima and Mojave. Yavapai was the biggest by far, and was basically the "Mother of Counties," constantly giving birth to new counties (including Coconino and Maricopa) for the next several years.

We may complain about the drought we seem to be currently experiencing, but back about 1150 AD, there was a mega-drought that lasted sixty years. The song that highlights snow, cold and Christmas was written by Irving Berlin one hot summer in 1940 while vacationing at the Arizona Biltmore in Phoenix.

Arizona has had a plethora of nicknames since statehood came about. Currently, the official name is "Grand Canyon State," but some of the former names include "Copper State," "Apache State," "Aztec State," "Baby State," "Valentine State," "Sand Hill State," and "Sunset State."

The first governor of the state was George W. P. Hunt, sometimes called George VII because he was elected seven times. Like President Taft, who signed the Enabling Act,

Hunt could be described as bit corpulent. He was 5'9" tall and weighed 300 pounds. Taft was 6' tall and weighed 330 pounds. Big men! Hunt was born in 1859 and died in 1934. Along with the seven terms he served as governor, he was president of the Arizona constitutional convention, served in both houses of the state legislature, and between gubernatorial sessions served as U.S. Minister to Siam. Not bad for a man who called himself the "Old Walrus." Politically he was a Democrat, (Republicans were almost as scarce as hens' teeth back then) a Progressive populist who was a strong supporter of women's suffrage, secret ballots, income tax, compulsory education, and organized labor. Although he came from a well-to-do Missouri family, he was definitely "blue collar." Hunt had left home while in his late teens (his family believed he had been killed by Indians) and made his way through the West until he found his way to Globe, Arizona. From there he made history.

Until recently Arizona was the only state with an official necktie: the bolo tie. Since then, both New Mexico and Texas have adopted the same official neckwear. In addition, Arizona has other "official" symbols. The cactus wren is our state bird; and, of course, the saguaro cactus blossom is the state flower. We have a state rattlesnake (Willard's rattlesnake), and an official raccoon (the ringtail) whose tail is longer than his body.

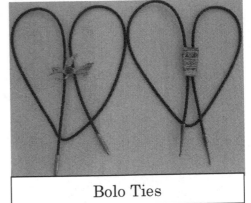

Bolo Ties

And to dispel a myth, the white man did not introduce Indians to alcohol. He did introduce them to *easier* alcohol...store bought. The Tohono O'odham and the Pima brewed some powerful beverages from fermented saguaro and fermented corn. To end with a bit of trivia...the first McDonald's franchise in the world opened in Phoenix in 1953.

ABOUT THE AUTHOR

Loretta Benore is a 19 year resident of the Village of Oak creek, Sedona Arizona. She has a B.A. in History and a M.S.S. in Social Science with emphases in both criminal justice and public policy. Her professional background is in domestic violence intervention and as the Crime Victim Compensation Program administrator in the First Judicial District Attorney's Office, Colorado. She has been a docent at the Sedona Heritage Museum since its opening in 1998 and is a former board member of the Sedona Historical Society. Loretta enjoys being a member of the Oakcreek Lady Niners Golf League, as well as being active in the Sedona Questers (and its historical players group) and the University Women of Sedona. (In the past she also served as a "conscripted" volunteer in her husband Dave's computer classes.)

Made in the USA
San Bernardino, CA
14 November 2017